Questions Non-Christians Ask

Barry Wood

Questions Non-Christians Ask

Fleming H. Revell Company
Old Tappan, New Jersey

Library of Congress Cataloging in Publication Data

Wood, Barry, date
    Questions non-Christians ask.

    Includes bibliographies and index.
    1. Apologetics—20th century. I. Title.
BT1102.W65   239   77-6280
ISBN 0-8007-0873-3 pbk.

Contents

Questions
Non-Christians
Ask

1

Can We Trust the Bible?

This is the age of skepticism. It is fashionable to doubt and question anything old, traditional, or historical. Often when sharing Christ with others, I hear the objection: "You keep saying, 'God says in the Bible . . . .' *Men* wrote the Bible, and I don't believe that it's 'God's Word.' It is full of errors and can't be trusted today."

When this statement is made about the Scriptures, how can the Christian respond constructively?

There is a basic question to ask any person who does not believe the Bible is God's Word. I ask, "Why do you *not* believe the Bible is God's Word?" Many times the unbeliever has no real basis for making such a statement. See if he can tell you exactly why he questions the authority of Scriptures. Then, if he has valid reasons for questioning the Bible, try to answer his questions. It is often true that he has not thought the matter through and has no real facts to support his statement.

It is good to discover where people are in their theology. I ask questions such as the following: "Do you believe God exists? If so, can He speak to mankind? If He can speak, how would He reveal Himself? Directly? Through men?"

The Bible answers all of hese questions. It claims to be God's Word, revealing God to men.

THE BIBLE CLAIMS TO BE GOD'S WORD

Repeatedly the Scriptures say, "Thus saith the Lord." In 2 Timothy 3:16 it says, "All Scripture is inspired by God and profitable for teaching, for reproof, for correction, for training in righteousness."

This Scripture tells us several things about the Bible:

It Is Inspired by God

The word *inspired* is, literally, "God breathed." Scripture is God breathed. It does not say the writers of Scripture were inspired, it says that what they wrote was inspired.

It Is Profitable for Us

Scripture is trustworthy. You can trust it to reveal God to you. It claims authority for itself to train us in righteousness. One other Scripture states clearly the Bible's claim to divine authority: 2 Peter 1:21, which says, ". . . no prophecy was ever made by an act of human will, but men moved by the Holy Spirit *spoke from God*" (italics added). These verses from Paul and Peter both state the divine origin of the Scriptures.

CAN THE BIBLE SUPPORT ITS CLAIM?

Many times I am asked, "You don't take the Bible literally, do you?" Now, there's a loaded question if I ever heard one. That's like asking, "Have you stopped beating your children?" Either way you answer, you're guilty! My answer is determined by your definition of *literally*. By *literally* I mean you must read the Bible seeking to understand the clear intention of the writer. He may use many symbols and figures of speech, but the literal meaning will be his obvious intention. Yes, I do take the Bible literally, especially when it claims to be God's Word—because I want to understand everything our great God has to say to me. If you doubt the Bible is God's Word, then let's put the Scriptures to the test.

WHAT ARE THE TESTS OF HISTORICAL ACCURACY?

Is the Bible mythical legend, comparable to *Beowulf*, or is it grounded and rooted in history? This question arises because the Bible has gone through many translations and languages. Even today, the multitudes of modern translations tend to add confusion to the uninformed about the accuracy of the Bible. Many unbelievers are actually convinced that the Bible contains so many significant errors it can't be trusted today. The task of the Christian witness is to show that this just is not true. We must show that the Bible is as true as any book of history. To begin with, how do you establish the reliability of any historical document?

There are three tests historians use to determine the reliability of ancient manuscripts, says C. Sanders in *Introduction to Research in English Literary History* (New York: MacMillan Co., 1952). These tests are: the *bibliographical test,* the *internal evidence test,* and the *external evidence test*. In the interest of brevity, we shall look only at the New Testament documents.

The Bibliographical Test

Since we do not have the originals of any book of the Bible, how reliable are the copies we have? This question is answered two ways: by the number of manuscripts and by the time interval between the original and the oldest existing copy. In witnessing it is not our purpose to give detailed thesis to any of this, but rather to give one good illustration of our point. If the person you are dealing with wants detailed information there is a wealth of material written on this subject.

Let's look at the bibliographical test for the reliability of the New Testament as it testifies to the historical Jesus. There exist today 13,000 manuscript copies of portions of the New Testament. There are 5,000 Greek manuscripts that contain all or part of the New Testament. So figures Bruce Metzger in *Text of the New Testament* (New York and Oxford: Oxford University Press, 1968).

John Warwick Montgomery, contemporary historian, says in his *History and Christianity* (Downers Grove, Illinois: InterVarsity Press, 1971), "To be skeptical of the resultant text of the New Testament books is to allow all of classical antiquity to slip into obscurity, for no documents of the ancient period are as well attested bibliographically as the New Testament."

Now, can this be illustrated? Yes, it can. Dr. F. F. Bruce in his notable book *New Testament Documents* has shown the comparison between the New Testament and ancient historical writings:

Perhaps we can appreciate how wealthy the New Testament is in manuscript attestation if we compare the textual material for other ancient historical works. For Caesar's Gallic War (composed between 58 and 50 B.C.) there are several extant MSS, but only nine or ten are good, and the oldest is some 900 years later than Caesar's day. Of the 142 books of the Roman history of Livy (59 B.C.–A.D. 17), only 35 survive; these are known to us from not more than 20 MSS of any consequence, only one of which, and that containing fragments of Books III–VI, is as old as the fourth century. Of the 14 Books of the Histories of Tacitus (c. A.D. 100) only four and a half survive; of the 16 books of his Annals, 10 survive in full and two in part. The text of these extant portions of his two great historical works depends entirely on two MSS, one of the ninth century and one of the eleventh.

The extant MSS of his minor works (Dialogus de Oratoribus, Agricola, Germania) all descend from a codex of the tenth century. The History of Thucydides (c. 460–400 B.C.) is known to us from eight MSS, the earliest belonging to c. A.D. 900, and a few papyrus scraps, belonging to about the beginning of the Christian era. The same is true of the History of Herodotus (B.C. 488–428). Yet no classical scholar would listen to an argument that the authenticity of Herodotus or Thucydides is in doubt because the earliest MSS of their works which are of any use to us are over 1,300 years later than the originals.

So, if the New Testament isn't accurate, reliable history, then there is no such thing as ancient history! This is only one test—the bibliographical!

The Internal Evidence Test

Again, can the New Testament pass this test? The internal evidence test has to do with authorship, style, et cetera to determine historical reliability. It was fashionable at the turn of this century to "prove" that the New Testament books were *not* written by the apostles but were written centuries later. The famous German liberal scholar Ferdinand Christian Baur declared that John's Gospel could not have been written until after A.D. 100 (at least sixty years after John's death!).

The John Ryland Manuscript In 1935, C. H. Roberts discovered a small piece of papyrus containing a few verses of John 18. It is now in the John Ryland Library, Manchester, England. Its date? Most scholars put it at A.D. 130! It is the oldest part of the New Testament discovered thus far. This "scrap" is no doubt a copy of the original or a copy of a copy of the original. Because it was discovered in Egypt, it attests to an early date for John's Gospel.

Eyewitness Testimony The New Testament writers claim to be eyewitnesses to the historical Jesus and His mighty works. It is good to show this internal evidence to any person who questions the validity of their witness.

LUKE 1:1–3 "Inasmuch as many have undertaken to compile an account of the things accomplished among us, just as those who from the beginning were eyewitnesses and servants of the Word have handed them down to us, it seemed fitting for me as well, having investigated everything carefully from the beginning, to write it out for you in consecutive order, most excellent Theophilus . . . ."

1 JOHN 1:3 "What we have seen and heard we proclaim to you also, that you also may have fellowship with us; and indeed our fellowship is with the Father, and with His Son Jesus Christ."

ACTS 2:22 "Men of Israel, listen to these words: Jesus the Nazarene, a man attested to you by God with miracles and wonders and signs which God performed through Him in your midst, just as you yourselves know—."

LUKE 3:1 "Now in the fifteenth year of the reign of Tiberius Caesar, when Pontius Pilate was governor of Judea, and Herod was tetrarch of Galilee, and his brother Philip was tetrarch of the region of Ituraea and Trachonitis, and Lysanias was tetrarch of Abilene . . . ."

The writers of the New Testament knew the value of firsthand testimony. Their witness was apostolic. They walked with Jesus. It was a powerful witness to the person of Jesus Christ.

The question is raised, Is their testimony reliable? Given the fact that the documents are authentic apostolic witness, are they an honest witness?

This question is valid and helpful. Because if the apostles lied, stretched the truth, or in any way embellished the truth about what they saw or thought Jesus to be, then we have reason to doubt their witness as to accurate history.

However, this was not the case. The New Testament writers were meticulously accurate *lest* they be attacked and exposed for fraud. Notice the documentation of facts by Peter at Pentecost. He said, "We are witnesses of these things . . . *as you yourselves know*" (*see* Acts 2:22). Their critics were everywhere. The Jewish rulers and Roman authorities would have delighted in exposing such a fraud as the Resurrection. Such exposure would have ended the Christian movement before it ever began. If the apostles lied about the miracle of Christ and His bodily Resurrection, there were thousands of living witnesses who could have contributed their testimony. But none did!

An illustration might help: Suppose I were to write a biography of John F. Kennedy. In that book, suppose I were to state that John F. Kennedy claimed to be the Messiah of the world and that he predicted his assassination in Dallas to his Cabinet. Not only that, but he prophesied to them his resurrection three days later. Now suppose I were to have that book published. What would happen? Among a number of things, both the publisher and I would be sued! Why? Because there are thousands of people living today who knew President Kennedy and who could and would refute my testimony. The book would gather dust on bookstore shelves and quickly be discounted as mythical. Not so with the New Testament records. None came forth to refute their testimony. As Paul said of the Resurrection, ". . . He appeared to more than five hundred brethren at one time . . ." (1 Corinthians 15:6). The Roman authorities would have been only too happy to have put a stop to the message of Jesus, if only it were possible. An empty tomb, a resurrected Lord, and a spirit-empowered Church were testimony too strong to overcome. The New Testament definitely passes the internal evidence test.

The External Evidence Test

Here is a different method of determining the accuracy, reliability, and authenticity of a document. Historians seek to find other sources which substantiate the literature under question. Again, the Bible is the world's most documented ancient literature:

The Early Church Fathers There exists today a vast amount of material written from the first century through the fourth century which is either knowledgeable of or quotes from the New Testament. Such men as Clement of Rome (A.D. 95), Ignatius (A.D. 70–110), Polycarp (A.D. 70–156), and Irenaeus (A.D. 180) along with many others recognize the New Testament as divine Scripture written by the apostles.

The Diatessaron Perhaps the first collection of the Gospels was put together by the Assyrian Christian Tatian (A.D. 170). Tatian organized the Scriptures and sought to harmonize the four Gospels. His work is called the *Diatessaron* and is recognized as a solid external evidence for the Scriptures as valid historical documents.

Archaeology Another external evidence to support Scripture as reliable is archaeology. The Bible has nothing to fear from investigation. The science of archaeology is the friend of Scripture. Every shovel that digs a hole in Bible lands will be used to authenticate the Bible. Many quotes are possible, but only two are necessary to make our point:

Nelson Glueck, renowned Jewish archaeologist wrote: "It may be stated categorically that no archaeological discovery has ever controverted a biblical reference." He referred to "the almost incredibly accurate historical memory of the Bible, and particularly so when it is fortified by archaeological fact." (*Rivers in the Desert, History of Neteg,*

Philadelphia: Jewish Publications Society of America, 1969.)

William F. Albright, world-famous archaeologist states: "There can be no doubt that archaeology has confirmed the substantial historicity of Old Testament tradition. As critical study of the Bible is more and more influenced by the rich new material from the ancient Near East we shall see a steady rise in respect for the historical significance of now neglected or despised passages and details in the Old and New Testament." (*From the Stone Age to Christianity,* Baltimore: Johns Hopkins Press, 1946.)

These are remarkable statements from very remarkable men. These men are the foremost authorities in their field. Can there be any doubt that the Scriptures *are* history? And, if they are history, then Jesus Christ is real. He then stands as the Lord of History and the Lord of Life, demanding worship and service from all men in every age. This is the issue we each must face: What shall I do with Jesus, the Christ?

THE TEST OF FULFILLED PROPHECY

A valid proof that the Bible is the supernatural Word of God is remarkable number of fulfilled prophecies it contains. These prophecies are not vague generalities given by some fortune-teller. They are very specific God-directed prophetic statements.

Deuteronomy 18:21–22 gives God's requirement for a true prophet. He must be 100 percent accurate. Therefore, if the Bible is God's Word, every fulfilled prophecy must be 100 percent correct. The Bible contains prophecies on many subjects, covering thousands of years. The most remarkable group of prophecies are those concerning the coming Messiah. These prophecies are very specific in describing the coming Savior who will save men from their sins.

The Address of the Messiah

A person's address is used to locate that specific person. An address can be very exact. For example, my address might be:

> John Doe
> 1001 Joy Street
> Dallas, Texas 76004
> United States of America

Note that this address tells you several things:

- It tells you I live on a certain continent on planet Earth.
- I live in the United States on that continent.
- I live in Texas in the United States.
- I live in a certain city in that state.
- I live on a certain street in that city.
- I live on a certain block on that street.
- I live on a certain lot on that block.
- I am a certain person, in that house on that block.

Now, that's getting specific! *The Bible is that specific about the address of the Messiah.*

The Old Testament was completed 350 years before Jesus of Nazareth was born. The Old Testament prophets testified to the coming of a Savior (Messiah) sent from Jehovah God. Jesus Christ claimed to be that Messiah (John 5:39). Let's see if Jesus fits the address of the Messiah:

GENESIS 3:15 *The Messiah is called the "seed of woman."* We are told in this first Messianic prophecy in the Bible that the Savior will be born of flesh into the human family. He will be a human being, not an angel or the like.

1 CHRONICLES 1:24 *The Messiah will be born of the lineage of Shem.* Noah had three sons: Shem, Ham, and Japheth. Shem, the oldest, is the ancestor of Abraham, from

whom the Messiah is promised. Thus, this ancestry eliminates half of the human race. The Messiah must come from Shem and his descendants.

GENESIS 12:1–3 *The Messiah will be of the lineage of Abraham.* Here is an even more definite promise. The promise God made to Abraham is the greatest Messianic hope in the Bible. The Messiah will be a descendant of Abraham.

GENESIS 49:9, 10 *The Messiah will come out of the tribe of Judah.* Abraham had two sons, Ishmael and Isaac. Isaac had two sons, Jacob and Esau. Jacob had twelve sons, and these twelve sons made up the Jewish nation. One of those sons, Judah, became the tribe of Judah. Here in Genesis 49, father Jacob makes a prophecy regarding his son Judah. He says that the Messiah will come through the tribe of Judah. "Shiloh" will come. *Shiloh* means "the Prince of Peace." Revelation 5:5 calls Jesus "The Lion of the tribe of Judah." The Messiah will be Jewish! From Judah's tribe.

ISAIAH 11:1, 2, 10 *The Messiah will come out of the lineage of Jesse.* Jesse (of the tribe of Judah) will be the father of King David. Jesse was also the grandson of Boaz and Ruth. What a prophecy! The Messiah must come through the loins of Jesse! That's a very specific address!

ISAIAH 9:6, 7; 16:5 *The Messiah must be a "Son of David."* Here we are told that the Messiah will be a direct descendant of David, son of Jesse (*see also* Matthew 1:1). The Messiah will sit on David's throne.

MICAH 5:2 *The Messiah will be born in Bethlehem, city of David.* This prophecy was written in the eighth century before Christ, yet it tells us the birthplace of the Messiah. He will be born in Bethlehem, city of David, because He is a descendant of David. *NOTE:* It took a decree from Caesar Augustus for a worldwide census to bring this prophecy to pass. Mary and Joseph, descendants of David, lived in Nazareth but went to Bethlehem for the census, at which time Jesus was born. How marvelous are the ways of God! Jesus, Son of David, was born in Bethlehem, fulfilling the prophecy.

DANIEL 9:24–26 *The Messiah will be born 483 years after the commandment to restore and rebuild Jerusalem.* This prophecy is the most specific in all the Scripture. It tells us when the Messiah will die! Let's examine this prophecy more closely. Daniel says "the Messiah will be cut off." This is a reference to the crucifixion of the Messiah (see Psalm 22). Here Daniel gives a very definite address of the Messiah. He must die 483 years after King Artaxerxes gave the decree to rebuild Jerusalem. This decree was given March 14, 445 B.C. (*see* Nehemiah 2:1–8).

In explanation of the "seventy weeks" of Daniel, 9:24–26: "Seventy weeks" refers not to seventy weeks of days, but weeks of years. Thus, seventy weeks equals seventy units of seven years. It is a reference to the Jewish sabbatical year. Once each seven years the land was to be left to rest for a year. Seventy weeks thus equals 70 times 7, which equals 490 years. Daniel 9:24–26 says that there will be 7 weeks and 62 weeks from the time of the decree to rebuild Jerusalem and the time the Messiah will be cut off. That's 69 "weeks," which equals 483 prophetic years. *Note:* A Jewish year is 360 days, or 12 months of 30 days each. 483 years equals 173,880 days. When did Jesus enter Jerusalem for the week of His death? He entered Jerusalem on the tenth day of Nisan in Passion Week, which was April 6, A.D. 32.

What then is the conclusion? The 69 weeks (483 years) began with the decree to rebuild Jerusalem, March 14, 445 B.C., and ended the week Christ entered Jerusalem, April 6,

A.D. 32. What a miraculous address! Only the God of Abraham, Isaac, and Jacob could bring this to pass.

Now, we ask a question: Who is the only person who could possibly fit this very definite address? Jesus of Nazareth! He fits all eight of these clues to the personage of the Messiah. Jesus said, "O foolish men and slow of heart to believe in all that the prophets have spoken!" (Luke 24:25).

DOES THE BIBLE PASS THE TEST?

Now, you must decide: Does the Bible match its claim to be God's Word? If it does, then it is God's message of hope and forgiveness for you. Jesus Christ wants to be your personal Lord and Savior. You and I must trust Him as Lord of Life.

This chapter is only a brief survey of a very detailed and complex study. Should the reader desire to do a full study in this area, I recommend the following books for consideration: *Archaeology and the Religions of Israel* by William F. Albright, Johns Hopkins University Press, 1952; *The Books and the Parchments* by F. F. Bruce, Fleming H. Revell Company, 1963; *The New Testament Documents: Are They Reliable?* by F. F. Bruce, InterVarsity Press, 1964; *Our Bible and the Ancient Manuscripts* by Frederick G. Kenyon, Harper Brothers, 1941; *History and Christianity* by John Warwick Montgomery, InterVarsity Press, 1971; *Evidence That Demands a Verdict* by Josh McDowell, Campus Crusade for Christ, 1972.

2

Jesus and the Intellectual

A true atheist is hard to find. I'm sure there is such a creature, but I've never met one. There are many people who call themselves atheists, but upon further examination one discovers they are not at all.

A few years ago I met a young intellectual on the campus of a major university. When asked if he believed in God he replied, "I'm an atheist." Impressed by his straightforwardness, I asked for his definition of an atheist. He said, "An atheist is a person who doesn't believe God exists."

I told him that I disagreed with his definition. "An atheist," I said, "is a person who has investigated all areas of reality—such as science, philosophy, anthropology, religion—and based upon his thorough investigation, has not found evidence for God's existence."

"Have you studied that much in your search for God?" I asked him.

"Well, no I haven't," he replied.

"Then, maybe you are an agnostic, rather than an atheist," I said.

"Yes, that's right; I'm an agnostic," my young scholar answered.

I then quizzed him further: "What is your definition of an agnostic?"

He said, "An agnostic is someone who doubts whether God exists."

I felt his definition was only partly correct, so I amplified it for him. "An agnostic doesn't just doubt if God exists, but rather he is a person who says, 'Based upon everything I have investigated so far, I doubt if God exists. However, I'm still searching and studying, and I'm still open to the possibility that He indeed does exist.' *That* is an agnostic," I explained.

"You see, an agnostic is a seeker after truth. Are you a seeker after truth?" I asked the now bewildered student. "Because, if you are, I'd like to show you some very concrete scientific evidence to establish the fact of God's existence."

After this brief discussion I was able to involve this young intellectual in a rational dialogue concerning God's existence. The following is an outline approach to explaining the kinds of rational evidence.

Our method will be an empirical deductive approach. As in all scientific methodology, we will start with that which can be examined. We'll start with the "given" and make logical deductions from our observations. In deductive reasoning we reason from the general to the specific.

THE UNIVERSE AS EVIDENCE

Now, what is the largest created reality known to man? The universe, of course. You can't get any bigger than that! What then can we learn about God's existence by observing the universe? Historically, there have been what are called the classical "arguments" for God's existence. Some of these merit consideration.

The ancient Greek philosopher Aristotle looked at the universe and made a deduction: It had to have a beginning. That's not a very brilliant deduction, because every child has asked the same question, How did the world begin? Yet, it is a good question. How *did* the universe begin? Aristotle surmised that all created reality was the result of cause and effect. The universe is an effect. It is created reality. Something had to cause it. He called that something *first cause,* "the unmoved mover." Whoever or whatever that first cause is, was "god" to Aristotle.

Now, will this deduction hold up today in our advanced technology? Aristotle's deduction is still a valid evidence for God's existence. Modern man has only two explanations for the origin of the universe.

The Cosmic Evolution Theory

This theory has various forms, but essentially it states that the universe derived from primeval "stuff," some elementary particles of gas, et cetera. However, this is no explanation at all (Aristotle was smarter than that). Why? Because whatever that primeval "stuff" was, it was an effect, something or someone *caused* it. It was only a secondary cause. Here then is the problem. Science can deal only with created reality. Science only observes *effects.* Science cannot observe uncreated reality—that which is outside the universe. So, if you asked what *caused* the elementary building blocks (primeval gases) of the universe, then science must admit it doesn't know. Science can only observe secondary causes. But the universe is here! What caused it? Its presence demands an explanation.

Genesis One: First Cause   God's Word states the principle of first cause: "In the beginning [before secondary causes] *God* . . ."! Genesis says there was God before there was anything. God *created* (caused) the universe— and the Hebrew word for *create* that's used in Genesis 1:1 is *bara.* It implies that God created "out of nothing."

In explaining first cause as evidence for God's existence it needs to be stated that to assert God as Cause in no way describes God's personality. If anything, it describes only God as eternal power. It says nothing of a "being" or of a personality—just eternal power or force. Aristotle's "unmoved mover" is a long way from being the God of the Bible!

The Evidence of Design Look at the universe again. Not only did it have a beginning, it is a structured *designed* universe. As science examines created reality, it observes the universe as having laws and "uniformity." In fact, science uses these laws as the basis of all scientific investigation.

In other words, when you look at the world you realize it *looks* like it was planned by a master architect. The universe looks more like an architect's blueprint than it does a child's scattered building blocks.

Many years ago as Albert Einstein, the famous atomic scientist, was moving toward the postulation of his now famous theory of relativity, he "discovered" God in the process. Einstein saw the many laws and structures of our universe and "knew" it was no accident. It was designed. Based upon two evidences—first cause and design—Dr. Einstein called God "Supreme Being." Notice that his description of God carries two ideas: *Supreme* represents the eternity of God—God's "uncausedness." This asserts God as the ultimate power behind all things. Secondly, he called God a *Being*. Why? Because this supreme power can think, plan, and design our incredible universe. There has to be a mind or intelligence behind the universe. Intelligence is a quality of personhood or being.

I agree with the eminent doctor. The Psalmist said it long ago: "The heavens declare the glory of God . . ." (Psalms 19:1 KJV).

The universe demands a creator for its existence. The atheist must think through these deductions. From the universe we have found two evidences for the existence of a Supreme Being, or Mind. This is a long way from the Christian God whom Jesus called our Heavenly Father. We are not ready for that yet. This Supreme Mind may or may not be a personable God. It may just be a force or intelligence wholly unconcerned with man. So, let's make some more deductions from observing the "given" and see what else can be learned about God.

MAN AS EVIDENCE

The universe is cold and often ruthless. We cannot find evidence for a "good" God through nature. We must look elsewhere. There is only one thing we can observe more closely than the universe. That one thing is man. We don't merely observe man, we *are* man. Here we have some inside information—we are knowledgeable. Let us examine man as a created effect and see what we can learn about the Creator. Man is the artistic handiwork of the Designer.

The Moral Law

As we look at man we find an interesting characteristic common to all men. It is the law of decent behavior. All men are conscious of this law of inborn morality. C. S. Lewis calls this the *Natural Law* in *The Case for Christianity* (The Macmillan Company, New York). For a fuller discussion of Natural Law, see part two of this fine book. Men everywhere in every culture are conscious of right and wrong. Lewis maintains that this characteristic of man is the clue to understanding the meaning of the universe.

The basic principle of the Law of Human Nature is that all men know instinctively they ought to be unselfish. We ought to do the *right* thing toward others. Nowhere in human history is selfishness a virtue. It is a universal standard of all human morality. Because it is universal, philosophers have called it a "law."

We must find the source of this human trait. If we can find its origin in nature, environment, or culture, then we have explained it as a learned experience. If we cannot explain it as a learned experience, then it is an inborn trait—and if it is indeed "natural" to man, then this feeling has to come from somewhere outside the universe and can be used to give us more information about the meaning of life.

Is the Moral Law Universal?

What about all the various cultures of man that reveal different moral codes? Don't they disprove moral law? No, they do not. As C. S. Lewis points out in his *Case for Christianity*, men have only slightly different moralities, not wholly different moralities.

> Men have differed as regards what people you ought to be unselfish to—whether it was only your own family, or your fellow countrymen, or everyone. But they have always agreed that you oughtn't to put yourself first. Selfishness has never been admired. Men have differed as to whether you should have one wife or four. But they have always agreed that you mustn't simply have any woman you like.

You see, the point isn't that cultural ethics vary, but rather that man worries about ethics at all. Man is ethical: He lives by a code. He may not know what it is, but the Moral Law is there.

Of course, men universally break the Moral Law. We know we ought to live a certain way, but we do not.

Isn't Moral Law Only Herd Instinct?

Can this standard be learned? Yes, it can—but that does not explain the instinct. Many human impulses are only responses to training and background. For example, a child can be taught to be unselfish. In that sense, unselfishness is learned. But this does not explain the hold that selfishness has on us.

For example, a person is drowning in a river and cries for help as you walk by. At that moment you will feel two desires: one a desire to help (due to your herd instinct), the other a desire to protect yourself (due to your instinct for self-preservation). At this moment, however, you will hear a third voice speaking inside you telling you that you ought to follow the impulse to help and suppress the impulse to run away. Now this third voice that tells you to choose one impulse above the other cannot itself be either one of the other two. This third voice is distinct and separate. It is the Moral Law and is quite different from the herd instinct.

As proof of this, the Moral Law usually tells you to side with the weaker of the two impulses. You probably want to run away more than you want to help the drowning person—but the Moral Law tells you to help him anyway.

Isn't the Moral Law Only Environmental?

Again, this law can be taught, but that doesn't explain its origin. A parent teaches a child that two plus two equals four. The child has learned a simple addition fact of mathematics. But this equation is a *law* of the universe. The parent has only *taught* a law; he has not *invented* a law. Of course, we learn the Law of Decent Behavior from parents and culture, as we learn everything else. The Moral Law, however, is not a mere human convention. It is in the same category as two plus two. Why?

First, because all cultures, with only slightly different variations, recognize this law.

And secondly, because we recognize one culture as being higher, more noble or more moral than another. We make such value judgments. For instance, we argue that Christian morals are higher than, say, Nazi morality.

The moment you say that one set of values is better than another, you are in fact comparing them by a standard, saying one of them more nearly conforms to this standard than the other. You are, in fact, admitting that there is really a right morality. Not just relativism, but a morality which is independent of what people think. There exists a RIGHT which is always RIGHT. This is the Moral Law.

So regardless of law, regardless of cultural standards, there is behind all behavior the consciousness of how we ought to behave. Now, if this sense of "oughtness" cannot be explained from training and environment, where did it come from?

Survival of the Fittest

One more explanation must be dealt with. Some have suggested that human beings recognize this principle of decent behavior in order that the race may survive. If people didn't behave decently toward one another, we would destroy human society. The argument is, you should behave decently so we can all live peaceably. You should be unselfish because man must live together and because we'll kill each other off if we don't obey the rules that are good for society in general.

My response is: "Why should I care if society survives? Why should I do what's best for others? It is survival of the fittest, isn't it?" The main problem with this reasoning is that it is double-talk. It reasons that I should be unselfish. I should behave unselfishly toward others because it will benefit *me*, and make *my* life more pleasant.

Sociologists say we should be ethical so society can survive. If we won't, we can't survive. Therefore all human ethics are only a convention, made necessary for the survival of the race. I am to behave well toward you so you will behave well toward me. However, how can I selfishly do unselfish actions? Why should I care what's good for society in general except when it happens to benefit me personally? But you say, "Because you ought to be unselfish." Which simply is double-talk. It still does not explain anything. It still does not tell me why I should be unselfish.

MORAL LAW AS A CLUE TO THE MEANING
OF LIFE

The Moral Law is there. It exists. It is real Law—none of us made it, but we find it calling us to live right, do right, and be right.

We are trying to "prove" the existence of God. We have used only two realities for our deductions: the universe and man. From the universe we conclude that He was a great artist, because the universe is such an awe-inspiring place, but also that He can appear quite merciless and no friend to man, because the universe can also be a very cruel and dangerous place. The other bit of evidence is that Moral Law which God has put into our minds. This inborn code is better evidence than the other because it is inside information. As C. S. Lewis says, "You'll find out more about God from the Moral Law than from the universe in general just as you find out more about a man by listening to his conversation than by looking at a house he has built."

This second evidence tells us that the Being behind the universe is vitally interested in right conduct, unselfishness, and love. This Being is moral, just, loving, and unselfish. This Being has given this divine trait to man. It then becomes a clue to the purpose of life. We are to live a certain way. We are to live by a standard. That standard is the very character of the Supreme Being. We are now approaching a description of the God of the Bible. The Bible describes God as a holy, loving, Creator. The Moral Law is our internal, personal witness to His existence. We cannot escape Him, because we cannot escape the Moral Law.

Goodness at the Wheel of the Universe

If the universe is not governed by a moral Being, then all human efforts at maintaining goodness are hopeless. But if it is, then we are making ourselves enemies to that absolute goodness every day, and we aren't likely to improve our conformity to that standard much tomorrow. We can't do without it, and we can't do with it. God is the only comfort, He is also the supreme tension. Love is at the heart of the universe, and we must do the loving thing or fail miserably as human beings. Make no mistake about it. God is there. He does exist. He expects us to live by His standard. This we cannot do in and of ourselves. This is why we need forgiveness.

Atheism Is Too Easy

These "evidences" are reasons why I say atheism is too easy. He who thinks through all the logical deductions that life demands just cannot settle for atheism. Atheism demands rebellion against the Moral Law and the universe. Atheism is not intellectual, it is immoral! Men do not reject God in their minds until they first reject Him in their hearts. The question of God's existence is not a mental question, it is rather a moral question. Every intellectual needs to realize this point. This is why we need to understand the Moral Law. It is proof that life does have meaning. It is proof that all men have failed to be what they ought to be. We are in need of forgiveness. It is at this point that the Bible speaks to every man.

The Bible's Personal God

The Bible tells us that the power behind the Moral Law is a merciful Father. He desires to forgive and guide us by His power. He is the God and Father of our Lord Jesus Christ.

It is this God that we Christians believe in. He is the God who became man in Jesus Christ to live out the moral standard of God for us. His life, death, and Resurrection offer us forgiveness and personal fellowship with the God who really does exist.

3

Isn't Christian Conversion Only Psychological?

I once met a brilliant college professor in search of reality. He is an engineer doing research at one of our major universities. When I first met him he told me he was an atheist. He was totally secular in his lifestyle and said he did not believe there was such a thing as altruistic love.

After much counseling and reading, he came to a point of crisis decision about the person of Jesus Christ. We prayed together in my home. He hesitantly invited Jesus the Christ to come into his life and be his Lord and Savior. He is today a changed man! He is now teaching Sunday school in a college department of his church. He has been "converted." How do you explain this radical reorientation of self? Can it be explained?

In September 1971 B. F. Skinner, noted psychologist, published his now famous book *Beyond Freedom and Dignity*. Skinner, a great behaviorist and educational psychologist, pictures man as a machine to be programmed and computerized. Skinner would probably explain away the "conversion" experience of this college professor. Why? Because everyone knows there is no God except in our minds as we project our "father needs" into an invented cosmic father in the sky. In Christ, is conversion a real experience of miraculous origin, or are the educational psychologists right? Is man only a pawn of chance on the chessboard of evolutionary history? This is a very real challenge to the evangelist, and you will face this challenge often as you witness to a secular society.

QUESTIONS PSYCHOLOGISTS RAISE

Before we discuss how to answer the psychologist, let's first review the current scene of B. F. Skinner's world. What explanations of Christian experience are we most likely to face?

Christian Experience Is Too Subjective to Be Valid

Some will cop out here and declare that one's personal experience is too subjective to test scientifically. They say it is unexplainable. However, the whole science of psychology is based on the premise that human behavior *is* explainable. That's what psychology is all about.

The Freudian Father Image

Older psychologists call Christian experience only wishful thinking. They say religion is man's response to an alien environment. Dr. Freud would say that man needs to feel that "somebody out there likes me." So, we "invent" God as a Father who cares. This always raises the question of which came first, man or God. It's kind of like the old riddle of which came first, the chicken or the egg. We Christians believe God created man with a need for Himself, and that is why man is religious.

Religion Is for the Emotional Cripple

A common explanation is that religion is like Linus's security blanket in the Charles Schulz comic strip *Peanuts*. Only the neurotic really needs a God. He is only for the weak and the emotional.

Conditioned Reflexes

Remember Pavlov's dog? The current scene in psychology is the field of experimental and educational research. Man is to be put into a laboratory, and examined like a rat. This view of man says everything man is and does can be determined by conditioned response. Even so with Christian conversion. People can be programmed to respond religiously, just as a rat can be programmed to ring a bell in order to get food.

IN DEFENSE OF REAL CONVERSION

How then do we validate the new-birth experience to a secular man who has come to disbelieve in a real love, real guilt, and a real God who forgives and changes human behavior?

Those who are opposed to religion for psychological reasons love to point out that religion is a major source of mental illness! We need to admit that there are emotional cripples who use God as a crutch. However, Christian conversion is not just "religion" or primitive superstition. Some people really do find God—not all, but some.

In Matthew 13 Jesus tells the story of the farmer who sowed seed in different kinds of soil. The soils represent differing responses people make to God. Not all of these responses are genuine "conversion" experiences. Jesus knew this and illustrated it for us.

The Intellectual Response

There are people whose religious faith is purely cultural and environmental. It is like a brainwashing. Jesus compared this to the seed that fell on the road. It had no root and it died. This is not true conversion; it is just environmental condition. We recognize this, as did Christ.

The Emotional Response

Jesus said some seed fell among rocky places where the soil had no depth. This is the person who has some shallow emotional experience with "God." God *is* his crutch. Then, when the emotion is gone, his need of God is gone. It doesn't last. Here again, we need to state that this is not what we mean by Christian conversion.

The Volitional Response

Jesus also described the person who makes a "decision" but fails to live up to it because the cares of the world choke his religious commitment as seeds are choked when planted among thorns. Many a person has been "converted" in some evangelistic crusade only to discover later that he got talked into something. Some people will join anything! We need to understand that this is not a true Christian.

Before true conversion happens, the total personality must be yielded to the Spirit of God. Dr. Orville S. Walters, a Christian psychiatrist, says that human personality is comprised of intellect, emotions, and will. He points out that the will is like a cart pulled by two horses named Intellect and Emotion. True conversion takes place only when mind and heart are yielded to His will. When the will is yielded to God, the whole self is changed. A valid Christian experience is a total, permanent, reorientation of a life. It is a seed planted in good soil bringing forth fruit a hundredfold.

DESCRIPTION IS NOT EXPLANATION

When someone tells me he can explain away conversion psychologically, I like to establish the difference between describing something and explaining *why* it happened. There is a difference! For example, a scientist may be able to describe the atom, but he cannot tell you why it's there. He can't explain its origin or its energy. A biologist can describe life, but he cannot explain it or tell you why it's there. So it is with the miracle of the new birth. Trying to explain all Christian experience by psychological terms just does not fit the facts.

The Unexplainable Explains Christianity. One of the great proofs that Jesus Christ is the risen Son of God is the radical change He makes in human lives. I've heard an ex-heroin addict state that experiencing Jesus Christ is the only cure for heroin addiction. How is this possible? God only knows! (Excuse the adaptation!) The alcoholic is converted, never to desire drink again. The homosexual immediately becomes heterosexual because he has met Christ. The guilt-ridden is freed from his prison of guilt and finds peace through the Prince of Peace. How are these things possible? These are challenges we must throw out to those who do not believe—because these changed lives are some of the greatest evidences that Christ is the risen Son of God.

One way to describe conversion is to explain what it is not:

Conversion Is Not Self-Improvement

It is not the power of positive thinking. Otherwise everyone who thought positive thoughts would live positive lives. Many a psychiatrist has offered advice he himself could not live by. Are psychiatrists happier than we "normal" folks? It remains to be seen. The suicide rate among physicians is considerably higher than among the general population—and among psychiatrists, it is higher still (*Identifying Suicide Potential,* Anderson and McLean, 1971).

Conversion Is Not Autohypnosis

Can true conversion be explained as merely self-hypnosis? Any subjective experience is hard to investigate. Someone may claim to have "seen" God in some ecstatic vision. How do you test the validity of such statements? We need some valid criteria to go by:

Have Others Had the Same Experience?   Here is our first criterion. Millions have had the same exact experience of receiving Jesus Christ, with the same profound results.

Paul Little tells of an experience of Harry Ironside, the great preacher. While Ironside was preaching, a heckler shouted, "Atheism has done more for the world than Christianity!"

"Very well," said Dr. Ironside, "tomorrow night you bring a hundred men whose lives have been changed for the better by atheism, and I'll bring a hundred who have been transformed by Christ."

That was the last Ironside ever saw of the heckler! (Paul Little, *Know Why You Believe.*)

Is Your Experience Based on a Demonstrated Objective Reality?   How does the Christian know he is not self-hypnotized? Because in Christianity our changed life is caused by the real presence of the risen Lord Jesus. He is real. He exists. He was seen by others. There is historical documentation of His life, death, and bodily Resurrection. (See chapter 1, "Can We Trust the Bible?" for further discussion.) In Christian experience, there can be no lasting change unless He (God) is the true source of it all. We profess that God is truly *there*.

Conversion Is Not a Conditioned Reflex

The statement that all Christian experience can be written off as environmental is a very weak argument. Why? Because many people became Christians whose parents are not. Many even go against culture to accept Christ. I have many Jewish friends who have experienced Jesus Christ and embrace Him in spite of social pressure and persecution from loved ones in their families.

Also, many people have been converted the very first time they were presented the gospel of Christ. They had no previous conditioning that can explain their transformation.

AFFIRM THAT JESUS CHRIST REALLY DOES CHANGE LIVES

There are some very basic needs that all men have, the weak as well as the strong. Modern man, like his more primitive ancestors, still faces guilt, loneliness, boredom, anxiety, and fear. Only the Living God can fill the emptiness in man.

A Psychologist Contradicts Himself

Several months ago a research psychologist, thirty-two years of age, called me on the phone. He has three Ph.D. degrees. He is steeped in experimental psychology. He has taught that there is no such thing as altruistic love, and that man is only an animal conditioned to respond.

He rejected his young wife's love, treated her so cruelly that she finally left him. In shock, he realized how much he really loved her. Ridden with guilt and loneliness, he reached out for help. After much counseling he asked Jesus Christ to forgive him and come into his life. His burden was greatly lifted. He experienced a love he had never known. He later said to me, "What I have experienced contradicts everything I teach in the classroom. I found I have needs that only God can meet."

Isn't that a remarkable statement? Coming from such a man as that, it is truly remarkable. When sharing with those who are influenced by modern psychology, we need to challenge them to see for themselves. Christian conversion is unexplainable without belief in the living Savior Jesus Christ. To believe in Him is to see guilt removed, forgiveness granted, and emptiness filled. We must point out the sufficiency of Christian experience to meet human need.

William P. Wilson, a former dean of clinical neurophysiology, explained conversion in an article in the October 1974 edition of *Decision,* Copyright by Billy Graham Evangelistic Association:

> Doing research in Christian experiences, I was impressed with what conversion achieved. In fact, I was astounded. Drunkards were turned into sober people; heroin addicts into nonusers; depressed people into well-regulated people; angry people into gentle, kind people; fearful people into brave people; self-centered, prideful people into humble, loving people. I was flabbergasted at what God could do, and decided there must be some way to apply God's principles to what I do . . . .
>
> The Lord showed me that being a Christian psychiatrist is learning how to present Christ as a healer, either by leading the patient to the point that Christian values and beliefs can take over or helping him to unravel his problems.
>
> As professor of psychiatry and chief of electroencephalography, I teach about a third of the time and practice a great deal. There are so many messed-up people in the world who need help.
>
> My main interest is serving Jesus Christ, and I praise the Lord every chance I get. My wife's faith has been renewed and our five children have come to know Christ. Our lives have so changed that we can witness to the world that Jesus Christ is Lord and that he lives! My life has meaning now. I have some-

thing to work for. To glorify God is the one great goal
in my life.

WHY PSYCHOLOGY CAN'T UNDERSTAND
CONVERSION

The Greek word *psyche* is translated "soul" in the Bible.
The word *psychology* comes from this word.

The Greek word *pneuma* is translated "spirit" in the Bible.

Man is made up of body, soul, and spirit. (*See* 1 Thessalonians 5:23.)

It is the spirit of man that is converted. A person is born
again in his spirit. This spiritual new birth changes the soul
(personality). All a psychologist can do is observe the
change in personality caused by the new birth. He can't
study the spirit in man, it's outside his field. In fact, most
modern psychology does not even recognize that man pos-
sesses spirit. This is why the phenomenon of Christian experience is impossible for the psychologist to comprehend.
In witnessing to people who have a background in these
sciences, I think we need to show them that man is more
than an animal and has profound spiritual needs that only
God can meet.

4

Won't a Good Moral Life
Get Me to Heaven?

Have you ever known a truly good person who was not a
Christian? Sure you have. There are many moral unbelievers who can "outlive" most Christians. How do you show
this person he needs a Savior? I once met a woman who
told me, "I don't need forgiveness, I've never sinned!" Although I had my doubts as to the validity of that statement,
there are those who feel they have earned heaven by their
good living. How can the Christian witness guide such a
person to his need of Jesus?

JESUS MEETS A MORAL MAN

John 3:1–7 tells of Christ's encounter with Nicodemus, a
devout rabbi among the Jews. Here Jesus meets the moral
man face-to-face. Nicodemus was a ruler among the Jews. A
Pharisee by profession, he is a classic example of a man
whose religion is the Ten Commandments.

As Nicodemus comes to Christ, giving him great compli-
ment as a mighty teacher from God, Jesus challenges him
(verse 3) with the words "Truly, truly, I say to you, unless
one is born again he cannot see the kingdom of God." (The
Greek word for "again" is *ana,* meaning "from above,"
which indicates a spiritual rather than a physical birth.)

Have you been born again? Have you experienced a

spiritual rebirth? This is Jesus' challenge to the moral man. This new-birth experience is God's requirement for salvation.

Morality Is Not Spirituality

Why do all men, regardless of how good they are, need to be born again spiritually? Because morality is not spirituality. We need to define some terms.

What Is Morality?

Morality means right relations with your fellow man. *Morals* refers to ethics on a man-to-man, person-to-person level. *Morals* denotes our horizontal relationships.

What Is Spirituality?

Spirituality means right relations with God. Being a spiritual man involves a daily walk with God. It denotes a vertical relationship—God to man, and man to God.

Therefore, morality is not spirituality. Not every moral man is right with God. There are many good, moral people—who wouldn't consider breaking the law or hurting one's neighbor—who are atheist by religious profession.

Robert Ingersoll, a celebrated atheist of a century ago, was a very moral man. Indeed, he was a philanthropist and humanitarian. So, being right with men doesn't make you right with God.

However, every spiritual man will be a moral man! This is the key to understanding Christ's challenge to Nicodemus. He who is born of God keeps himself from sin, John says in his first Epistle. Dr. Nicodemus is a good illustration of a moral person who was not right with God.

WHY CAN'T A GOOD MORAL LIFE SAVE YOU?

A moral life can't save you because God's standard of righteousness is too high. What is God's standard of morality? It is the Ten Commandments as taught by the Sermon on the Mount and lived out through the life of Jesus Christ. In other words, God's standard of morality is Jesus Christ. How good is good enough to please God? As good as Jesus! That's how good—sinless perfection! What an incredible requirement!

Jesus said, "I do *always* those things that please the Father" (*see* John 8:29). He said again, "Which of you accuses Me of sin?" (*see* John 8:46).

Who's Perfect?

If a man is to be saved by works, he would have to be perfect even as Christ was perfect. James 2:10 says, "For whoever keeps the whole law and yet stumbles in one point, he has become guilty of all." Paul says in Galatians 5:3, "And I testify again to every man who receives circumcision, that he is under obligation to keep the whole Law." Circumcision refers to those who choose to be saved by means of good works. If this is how you choose to be saved, then your goal is perfection. If you stumble once, you are guilty of all. You are obligated to keep the whole law of God.

How Good Are You?

Suppose you commit only one sin a week in thought or deed. (Remember your measuring rod is the Ten Commandments as lived and taught by Jesus!) That's fifty-two sins a year. If you live a normal lifetime of seventy years, you will have committed 3,640 sins! Can you imagine if you had committed 3,640 crimes and were finally caught and tried? What do you think the verdict would be? Guilty or innocent? Why, the judge would lock you up and throw away the key! Can you see how your righteousness must look to a holy God, the Judge of heaven and earth? Romans 3:10 says it well: "There is none righteous, no, not one" (KJV).

WHY DID JESUS DIE ON THE CROSS?

Jesus told Nicodemus that the Son of Man must be lifted up on a cross to die for the sins of the world. (*See* John 3:14, 15.)

Now I ask you a question: If anyone could ever be good enough to be saved by his own good deeds, then why did God nail His beloved and innocent Son on a cross? Christ's death for *all* men is senseless if all men are not in need of this substitutionary death.

- You are your own savior if you are trying to get to heaven by your own works. Because you cannot fulfill God's requirements, you need a Savior who can meet His requirements.
- Jesus Christ was sent by God to keep the law for us and to give His life for our sins. (*See* Luke 19:10 and Romans 5:8.)
- All men need to be born again through faith in Christ. This is Christ's message to Nicodemus. Jesus Himself is our only hope of pleasing God. To accept Him is to have God accept you. If you do not accept God's Son, God will never accept you. Jesus concluded His talk with Nicodemus by saying, "He who believes in the Son has eternal life; but he who does not obey the Son shall not see life, but the wrath of God abides on him" (John 3:36).

WHAT IS GOD'S WAY OF SALVATION?

Read carefully Romans 3:20–24. Here is a clear statement that no one can be forgiven of sin by being good. God does not grade on the curve! It's all or nothing. God offers us a better way of salvation. It is not dependent on our works but upon the sinless life of the Lord Jesus. God, through Christ, offers fellowship with Him as a free gift in Christ. (*See also* Ephesians 2:8–9 and Titus 3:5.)

YOU CAN'T MAKE IT ON YOUR OWN

Perhaps further illustrations are needed to clarify this point. Paul Little shares the following illustrations:

Suppose the entire human race lined up on the West Coast with one objective, to get to Hawaii. We'll equate their goal with God's standard of righteousness. The gun is fired and all the swimmers jump in. As we look down over the ocean we see the most moral of all. He's been a wonderful professor and a good man, always doing his best and following high moral standards; yet he would be the first to admit his imperfection and sinfulness. But he's out there in the water seventy-five miles from shore. Next we pick out the Joe College fellow who's not quite ready for Sing Sing or Cook County Jail. He does cheat on exams a little and goes on a binge now and then; he gets into a few scrapes and does things that are wrong. But he's not really too bad. He's gotten about ten miles out. A derelict from Skid Row is practically drowning one hundred and fifty yards offshore. Scattered about in the water between the two extremes of the spectrum we see the rest of the human race. As we look from the bum on Skid Row to the Joe College type to the tremendously moral man who's gone seventy-five miles, we see the difference. It's an enormous difference. But what's the difference in terms of Hawaii? Everyone will drown.

> *How to Give Away Your Faith*
> (InterVarsity Press, 1966)

It's obvious that swimming lessons won't help. The goal is unreachable. You'd just as well try to swim to Hawaii as try to reach heaven by yourself. All religions in the world are essentially sets of swimming lessons, suggesting codes of ethics to live by. Yet our problem isn't knowing how to live; our problem is in finding the resources to live the way we ought. That's where Jesus Christ comes in. He and He alone can meet God's requirements, and He and He alone can forgive our sins and fill our life with joy and meaning.

5

Why Are There So Many Hypocrites?

Every Christian witness has heard this objection in one form or another. Many times an unbeliever will observe the rotten life of some carnal Christian and say, "Well, I'm as good as So-and-So, and he goes to your church every Sunday." Another version of this statement is: "I'll become a Christian when all those hypocrites get out of the Church."

In responding to the hypocrisy question it is always good to know the motive of the person who asks it. If the question is asked in a proud, boastful spirit, then you're better off not answering it. However, an unbeliever has often been truly disappointed by the behavior of some church member, and this is a real barrier keeping him from becoming a Christian. If this is the case, I believe the issue can be clarified rather easily.

WHAT IS A HYPOCRITE?

I agree with anyone who says there are too many hypocrites in the Church. If there is just one in any church, that is one too many!

However, when you say *hypocrite*, just what do you mean? If you mean a Christian who lives like the devil then maybe we need to define what a hypocrite really is. God's children are blamed for many things they don't do. Is the hypocrite a Christian? No, not by definition he isn't.

The Greek word that is translated *hypocrite* literally means to answer, to talk back. It was used to describe actors in ancient Greek drama who wore masks and spoke through these masks in dialogue to one another. The word came to mean one who is playacting or pretending to be something he is not.

Jesus and the Hypocrite

Christ is the only one to use the word *hypocrite* in the New Testament. He used the word to describe people who pretend to know God when they really don't. In Matthew 7 He describes the hypocrite. He says the way to tell a tree's inner nature is to look at its fruit, and the way to tell a real Christian from a false Christian is to look at his fruit (his life). Jesus then says, "Not every one who says to Me, 'Lord, Lord' will enter the kingdom of heaven; but he who does the will of My Father who is in heaven. Many will say to Me on that day, 'Lord, Lord, did we not prophesy in Your name, and in Your name cast out demons, and in Your name perform many miracles?' And then I will declare to them, 'I never knew you; DEPART FROM ME, YOU WHO PRACTICE LAWLESSNESS' " (verses 21–23).

Jesus is describing the true hypocrite. He is not a Christian, but he is in the Church doing religious work. He is a pretender, he is playacting. But Jesus isn't fooled and neither should you be. Jesus said of the hypocrite, "I never knew you."

In the Church but Lost

A person can be in the Church and not know God. It was religious people, the Pharisees, who crucified Jesus Christ. He called them hypocrites. Many times when you see some church member living a shameful life of sin you are not seeing a true Christian at all, just a hypocrite playing religion.

PITY THE HYPOCRITE, BUT DON'T JUDGE HIM

If you think there are too many hypocrites in the Church, you are right. However, the hypocrite is to be pitied. He is lost and doesn't know it. At least you as a non–church member admit you are an unbeliever. You know where you stand. You aren't deceiving yourself or anybody else. But pity the poor deceived fellow who thinks he's right with God and will die only to hear Jesus say at the Judgment, "Depart from me, I never knew you!" My point is: The hypocrite doesn't belong to the real Church. He is a lost Church member.

REMEMBER, THE CHURCH ISN'T PERFECT

Even as there are lost people on our church rolls who are not real Christians, it must be stated that genuine Christians can sin and fail God. Christians aren't perfect. If you'll remember, Jesus had twelve disciples. These men comprised the early Christian Church. Of these twelve men one betrayed Him (Judas, a true hypocrite), one denied Him, and another doubted Him. The other nine hid behind locked doors before the Resurrection. That's not a very good start for the Christian movement! Christians have never been perfect, nor do we claim to be.

What Is a Christian?

Being a Christian is not a claim to having "arrived." We are not supersaints sitting in judgment on the rest of the world. We ought to put signs over the doors of our churches which read, WELCOME: SINNERS ONLY, because that's the only kind of people there are. The only real difference between a saved sinner and a lost sinner is that the saved sinner has Christ helping him overcome temptation. But what a difference Jesus makes!

The Carnal Christian

Paul wrote to the Christians of Corinth, ". . . for you are still fleshly. For since there is jealousy and strife among you, are you not fleshly, and are you not walking like mere men?" (1 Corinthians 3:3). Here is the carnal, "fleshly" believer. Notice, they behave like "mere men." So, I encourage you not to keep your eyes on Christians but to fix your attention on Jesus. He never fails. It is He who is working in the lives of His people, making them more like Himself. Yet it is a process, and even the best of Christians will fail from time to time.

INVITE THE UNBELIEVER TO COME HELP CHANGE THE CHURCH

I encourage you to come follow Christ and help improve the Church by being a better Christian than any you've seen. Rather than stand in judgment of the hypocrite, why not give yourself to Jesus and show the world what it really means to follow the Savior. Luke 9:23 is a real challenge Jesus gave: ". . . If any man will come after me, let him deny himself, and take up his cross daily, and follow me" (KJV).

Missing the Point

Finally, I want you to understand that you should not miss knowing Jesus because of someone else's failure. The hypocrite isn't worth missing heaven for. Don't let Satan keep you from Christ's love by filling your heart with bitterness and resentment. He'll win and you'll lose. Judging others won't spare you the judgment of God.

Romans 2:1 says, "Therefore, you are without excuse, every man of you who passes judgment, for in that you judge another, you condemn yourself; for you who judge practice the same things."

6

Jesus and the Jew

I saw a bumper sticker the other day, JEWS FOR JESUS. I was amazed, because it was such an unusual concept. Jews and Jesus haven't gotten together in a long time. Yet why not? Jesus was a Jew! The religion that follows His teachings is very Jewish. Some of Christianity's sacred books, the Gospel according to Matthew and the Letter to the Hebrews, for instance, were written to Jews. In fact, all of Jesus' disciples were Jews, as was the early Christian Church. Early Christian-Jews originally worshiped Jesus as their Messiah in the synagogue.

Many Jewish people today are unaware of the cultural ties between Christian and Jew. This has come about for several reasons. Consider:

THE CREDIBILITY GAP

Many modern-day Jews do not trust Christians because of Jewish persecution by Gentiles. Some of this anti-Semitism has come in the form of organized Christian religion. For example, Jews were exterminated in Germany by a German government in a nation that was predominately Lutheran; many Jews, then, blame Christianity for the genocide of German Jews. Also, the Roman Church in Spain has in times past been very anti-Semitic. So you see, the Christian's credibility is in question among many Jewish people.

It must be stated, however, that no real follower of Jesus would ever persecute *any* race of people, much less our brothers of Israel. Jesus taught His followers the way of love. He is the Prince of Peace, and He wants us to live peaceably with all men. Jesus teaches us to pray for the peace of Jerusalem.

Also, many Christians have died protecting Jews from those who would destroy them. History validates the heroism of Dietrich Bonhoeffer in Germany, who opposed Hitler at the cost of his life. Corrie ten Boom and her family in Holland have shown the world that the friends of Jesus are also friends of Israel.

Modern Jews must not blame Christians for everything done against them by organized religion, any more than we Christians today can blame all Jews for the crucifixion of Christ. This is nonsense!

The God of Abraham, Isaac, and Jacob does not want Jew and Christian to be at odds. God's Messiah is for all men. The apostle Paul said, "For He Himself is our peace, who made both groups into one, and broke down the barrier of the dividing wall" (Ephesians 2:14).

Yet Jew and Christian are divided. A wall does exist. How can we as Christians help the Jew to accept our credibility?

- *Win His Trust*
  You must earn your Jewish friend's confidence. Love him!
- *Become His Friend*
  You must not seek to "convert" him to be a Christian. The word *convert* is a loaded word to the Jew. It means you want him to give up his Jewishness and become a Gentile. Treat him as a friend, not a prospect.
- *Show Him Messiah Has Come*
  Messianic Judaism is a live option for the Jew. His faith in Jesus as the Jewish Messiah will give him an even greater appreciation for his Jewishness and will complete his faith, not subtract from it.

THE COMMUNICATION GAP

Communication is the key. Many religious words we use are foreign to the Jew, even as his religious words are foreign to us. Some words need to be avoided, others need to be translated. A few examples:

SINNER   The Bible calls all men "sinners." Yet to the average Jew only Gentiles are sinners. The Jew is God's chosen, all else are sinners. So when you tell a Jew he is a sinner he doesn't think of the word as moral, but rather as ethnic. You must show him from *his* Scripture that he has broken God's laws and needs forgiveness. See Genesis 6:5 and Isaiah 64:6, 7. Until we see ourselves as guilty before the righteous Judge of heaven and earth, we'll recognize no need of a Savior Messiah.

CHRISTIAN   Never ask a Jew to become a Christian. Most Jews tend to think all Gentiles are Christians. To say that all Gentiles are Christians is no more true than to say that all Jews are orthodox believing Jews. They are not. Many Jews are agnostic. Especially is this true of the young Israeli.

The word *Christian* is too vague to communicate much of anything. I never ask anyone if he or she is a Christian, especially a Jewish person. The Jew understands *Messiah* better than *Christ*. *Christ* is the Greek equivalent of the Hebrew word *Messiah;* therefore, talk to Jewish people about Messiah. When he accepts YEHOCHUA HAMASHIACH (Jesus the Messiah) he becomes *more* Jewish. He is a fulfilled Jew, not a "Christian" as he understands it.

LOST   The Jew doesn't feel he is lost to God's will. Jews have always had a sense of history and purpose. Therefore, he doesn't understand Jesus' words "I came to seek and to save that which was lost" (*see* Luke 19:10). We must help him understand what this "lostness" is. We must explain it in Jewish terms he can understand.

SAVED   This word is often confusing to any unbeliever. Saved from what? Most Jews haven't the slightest idea—yet they need salvation. In fact, the Hebrew word for salvation is the word from which *Jesus* derives. Jesus *is* salvation. Paul said, "For I am not ashamed of the gospel, for it is the power of God for *salvation* to every one who believes, *to the Jew first* and also to the Greek" (Romans 1:16, italics added). Salvation is of the Jews. We must help the Jew to see his need of his Savior.

CHRIST   Regrettably *Christ* is a curse word for many people. It is a very Gentile term. Remember that *Christ* is the English rendering of the Greek *Christos,* meaning anointed one. *Christos* is the Greek rendering of the Hebrew word *Messiah.* Let's talk to the Jew about his Messiah, not our Christ.

THE CULTURE GAP

Here is what really separates Jew and Christian. Millions of Jews would turn to Jesus as Messiah overnight if it were not for the dividing wall of culture.

Fiddler on the Roof begins with Tevye singing the famous "Tradition." Tradition! This is the very heartbeat of Judaism. Judaism *is* tradition.

Every Christian who desires to share the Scriptures with the Jew must respect and comprehend this vast culture gap. This is the greatest barrier for the Jew. For him to come to Jesus as his Messiah is a noncultural, nontraditional, thing to do.

However, Judaism has changed and is changing. The theme of *Fiddler on the Roof* expresses the fact that traditions change with the shifting of the social current.

There are now no less than five different traditions among Jews, all calling themselves Judaism: Orthodox, Conservative, Reform, Zionism (Israeli culture), and Biblical Messianic Judaism. Strictly speaking, Zionism is not a "tradition" within Judaism. It is a movement back to the Promised Land supported by Jews worldwide. (This return was prophesied in the Scriptures centuries ago by Moses and other prophets.)

Now, ask your neighborhood rabbi which tradition is correct. Who's to say? Maybe *none* is! In fact, multitudes of young Jews have left the synagogue never to return, simply because there was little vital content for them.

Biblical Judaism

Many Jews hold to the one tradition which predates all the others—biblical Messianic Judaism, which believes that Jesus of Nazareth, Israel's greatest prophet, is the promised Messiah.

For two thousand years, there have been Jews who have followed this tradition. These Jews proclaimed to the world that the Messiah was promised *to* the Jews and came *as* a Jew, *through* a Jewish woman, *to* the Jewish people. His followers were Jewish and their Scriptures were Jewish. Then when Israel as a nation persecuted them (Jews persecuting Jews, by the way), these Jewish believers took Messiah to the Gentiles.

Which Tradition Is Judaism?

All of them are! But not all of them are the faith of Abraham, Isaac, and Jacob! The Jew should ask himself, "Is my life pleasing to God, or is it pleasing only to my rabbi and family?" It is the conclusion of many famous Jews that Messianic Judaism, which finds Jesus to be its Savior, is real Biblical Judaism.

SAUL OF TARSUS Saul (Paul) believed Jesus to be his Messiah. Friedrich Nietzsche characterized Saul as "that eternal Jew *par excellence.*" Yet how many modern Jews have read the writings of this great Jewish mind? He wrote one half of the New Testament!

FELIX MENDELSSOHN-BARTHOLDY Mendelssohn was born in Hamburg, the grandson of the great Moses Mendelssohn, philosopher and reformer. Before he was eighteen he produced his famous overture to *A Midsummer Night's Dream*. At thirty-seven he wrote the incomparable oratorio *Elijah*. Mendelssohn was a Jew who believed in Jesus as his Messiah and was proud of his Jewishness.

SAMUEL ISAAC JOSEPH SCHERESCHEWSHY Schereschewshy was founder of St. John's University, Shanghai, and translator of the Bible into the Mandarin and Wenli dialects. Max Müller, philologist, Oxford University, said of this great Christian Jew, "Bishop Schereschewshy was one of the six most learned orientalists in the world." Bishop Schereschewshy was a great Jew who loved Jesus.

We could go on and on. The roll call is large. For 2,000 years Jews have given Jesus to the Gentile world. He is their Messiah. The Bible is their book.

Why Doesn't Organized Judaism Accept Jesus As Messiah?

This is a good question. First of all the nation of Israel did *not* reject Jesus as Messiah. The people heard Him gladly and wanted to crown Him king. It was the religious hierarchy of Judaism that rejected Him. The apostle John testifies to this fact in John 12:42:

> However, even many of the Jewish leaders believed him to be the Messiah but wouldn't admit it to anyone because of their fear that the Pharisees would excommunicate them from the synagogue. (LB)

Isadore Lhevinne was correct in saying, "There remains this amazing, and so frequently overlooked truth: it is a lie that the Jews have rejected Christianity. Only a portion of Jews have rejected it. Had it not been for that heroic band of early Jewish disciples of Jesus, there would have been no Christianity now."

If you are Jewish, will you consider the possibility that Jesus could be the long-awaited Messiah? Let's ask some questions that need answering.

EVERYTHING YOU ALWAYS WANTED TO KNOW ABOUT JESUS BUT WERE AFRAID TO ASK YOUR RABBI

Question: Why don't most rabbis believe that the Messiah is a personal individual rather than a symbol of a future age of peace?

Answer: Because if they believe the Messiah is personal, then they'll have to interpret all of the Messianic passages in the Old Testament literally. And if they do that, then the Old Testament is like a road map leading to Jesus of Nazareth. He fulfilled over 300 Jewish prophecies.

For example, in the traditional prayer book that many conservative and orthodox synagogues use—*Daily Prayers,* translated by Dr. A. Th. Phillips—there is a reference to a *personal* Messiah. In a prayer for the return of the Messiah it says:

> . . . to Jerusalem, Thy city, return in mercy, and dwell therein as thou hast spoken; rebuild it soon in our days as an everlasting building, and speedily set up therein the throne of David . . . speedily cause the offspring of David, Thy servant, to flourish, and let his horn be exalted by Thy salvation, because we wait for Thy salvation all the day.

Now, does that prayer sound like a prayer for some vague future age—or a prayer for a personal Savior-Messiah, the *offspring* of David, to come and set up a kingdom?

It's interesting too, that the Hebrew word used here for *salvation* also translates JESUS.

Which Prayer Book Is Right?

Most rabbis, except some orthodox, would not interpret this prayer literally to refer to Messiah as an individual. What's even more confusing is that many Reform Jews use another version of the prayer book in which they have deleted all references to a personal Messiah and the rebuilding of the temple! Now, who gave them permission to delete holy Scripture from the prayer book just because it does not agree with their theological persuasion? It seems that there is no consensus of opinion among the rabbis even on the prayer book. What often passes for Judaism today has no more relation to authentic Biblical Judaism than Unitarianism has to New Testament Christianity.

Question: Why is Isaiah 53 ignored in the haftarah readings in connection with the Pentateuchal lesson?

Answer: Because Isaiah 53 is too controversial to explain away! Isaiah 53 is the hallmark of all Messianic prophecy. Yet most synagogues are strangely silent on this great prophecy. Few Jews even know its contents. Why? Because this chapter refers repeatedly to a person, not the nation (Israel). Even a casual reader will observe that Isaiah makes fifty-one references to a personal Messiah, not Israel. Isaiah says "He" will redeem "my people" (*see* Isaiah 52:14, 53:8, 11). Read Isaiah 52:11 through 53:12 and see for yourself. Then read Isaiah 54 and see the blessing that is to come to *Israel,* the nation, because of the Messiah.

A Strange Synagogue Prayer

It is little known how Oz M'lifnai B'reshis, one of the prayers for Yom Kippur, came to be incorporated into the Jewish Prayer Book. Some students of Jewish liturgy are of the opinion that the prayer is a Judeo-Christian infiltration into the poesy of the synagogal liturgy. Otherwise, what explanation is there for this strange petition from Musaf l'Yom Kippur:

Our righteous Messiah has departed from us. We are horror-stricken and have none to justify us. Upon his shoulders he carried our sins, and through his wounds we find forgiveness. O, Eternal One, create him anew. From Seir let come the Redeemer, from Mt. Lebanon let him proclaim redemption a second time through thy servant.

Would the poet have voiced the above had he not felt that the prophecy of Isaiah 53, mirroring the great Sufferer of the human race who brings redemption through His vicarious atonement, had been fulfilled in Jesus?

Why then is this fact kept from us? Yet there it stands, the choicest gem, the truest portrait of our Messiah in the whole prophetic volume!

Question: If Messiah isn't an individual, then why do the Scriptures repeatedly refer to Messiah as God's "son"?

Answer: Read Proverbs 30:4:

Who has ascended into heaven and descended?
Who has gathered the wind in His fists?
Who has wrapped the waters in His garment?
Who has established all the ends of the earth?
What is His name or His son's name?
Surely you know!

Is there any doubt this passage refers to Jehovah God and His "son"?

Psalms 2:2 refers to the Lord (Adonai) and His Messiah. Then in verses 7 and 8 the Messiah is called God's Son who will rule the nations. This and other references clearly teach Messiah is God's anointed, His Son. Jesus of Nazareth claimed to be that only begotten Son, and the rabbis of His day tried to reject Him for making such a claim!

Question: Did Jesus fulfill *all* of the Old Testament Messianic prophecies?

Answer: Jesus said, "You search the Scriptures, because you think that in them you have eternal life; and it is these that bear witness of Me" John 5:39. (*See also* Luke 24:25.) Jesus claimed to fulfill the Scripture. Did He? How much so?

Perhaps the greatest proof that Jesus is indeed the Jewish Messiah is the fact that He fulfilled *all* the Old Testament qualifications for God's Anointed One. Deuteronomy 18:21, 22 gives the test of a true prophet. This test requires 100 percent accuracy. There are over 300 prophecies regarding the coming of the Messiah. If Jesus is a true prophet, and truly the Redeemer of Israel, he had to fulfill them all. (For further discussion, see chapter 1, "Can We Trust the Bible?"—particularly the section headed *The Address of the Messiah.*)

JESUS PLANNED IT ALL

Some say that Jesus was a super-Einstein who just worked all of this out to fit Himself into this Messianic address—the eight Old Testament prophecies concerning the birth of Jesus cited earlier. What are the odds on Jesus' fitting into this scheme? Someone has calculated that the odds against Jesus' making all eight of these come true are *ten to the seventeenth power.* How great is that? Suppose you were to stack silver dollars two feet high and cover the state of Texas with them—and only one of them is marked with an *X*. Now suppose at random, quite by chance, you were to pick out the one with the *X* on the first try! What are the odds against your doing that? The odds are *ten to the seventeenth power.* These are exactly the odds that Jesus of Nazareth could not have just plotted and schemed and planned His life to fit the miraculous address of the Messiah which was written hundreds of years before He was born!

THE MESSIAH IN PROPHECY

The *Address of the Messiah* given in chapter 1 is only a brief presentation of Hebrew prophecy regarding the coming of the Messiah. There are over 300 references to the Messiah in holy Scripture.

The Old Testament reveals two very distinct portraits of the Messiah. He is Suffering Servant and Reigning King. Rabbis were so confused over this that many taught there would come two Messiahs. One will come and die for the sins of the people, and the other will come to rule forever over His people. I feel the Bible speaks of Jesus as both Suffering Savior and Lord of Lords.

He suffered first, and will come again to reign at the end of the age. For the person who desires a more thorough study of this subject, here is a more comprehensive list of prophecies:

Two Portraits of the Messiah

Reigning King	*Suffering Servant*
Psalms 2:6–8	Psalms 22:18
Psalms 68:18	Psalms 69:21
Psalms 118:22	Isaiah 50:6
Isaiah 9:6, 7	Isaiah 52:14
Isaiah 42:1–4	Isaiah 53:1–10
Jeremiah 23:5	Zechariah 11:12
Daniel 2:44	Zechariah 12:10
Daniel 7:13, 14	Zechariah 13:7
Micah 5:2	
Zechariah 6:12, 13	
Zechariah 9:9, 10	
Malachi 3:1	

Here too is a list of Old Testament prophecies, along with the historical fulfillment of each in the life of Jesus the Nazarene:

Old Testament Prophecy		New Testament Fulfillment
Genesis 3:15	Seed of woman	Galatians 4:4
Genesis 49:10	Born to the tribe of Judah	Luke 3:33
Isaiah 9:7; 11:10	Heir to David	Matthew 1:1
Micah 5:2	Bethlehem to be place of birth	Matthew 2:1
Daniel 9:25	Time of birth	Luke 2:1, 2
Isaiah 7:14	Virgin birth	Matthew 1:18
Hosea 11:1	Flee to Egypt	Matthew 2:14
Deuteronomy 18:15	He will be a prophet	John 6:14
Isaiah 11:2	Anointed of God	Luke 2:52; 4:18
Psalms 2:2–12	Son of God	Matthew 3:17
Malachi 3:1–3	John the Baptist	John 1:19

Events Surrounding Death of Christ

Old Testament Prophecy		New Testament Fulfillment
Zechariah 9:9	The King will come on a donkey	John 12:13, 14
Psalms 41:9	Betrayed by a friend	Matthew 26:14, 15
Zechariah 11:12	Money paid	Matthew 26:15
Zechariah 11:13	Potter's field	Matthew 27:7–10
Isaiah 53:7	Silent when accused	Matthew 26:62, 63
Isaiah 50:6	Beaten and spat upon	Mark 14:65
Isaiah 53:4, 5	A substitutionary death	Mark 10:45
Isaiah 53:12	Crucified with sinners	Matthew 27:38
Psalms 22:16	Crucifixion	John 20:27
Psalms 69:21	Gall and vinegar to drink	John 19:29
Psalms 22:7, 8	Mock the Messiah	Matthew 27:43
Zechariah 12:10	Side would be pierced	John 19:33
Psalms 22:18	Cast lots for garments	Mark 15:24
Psalms 34:20	Not a bone broken	John 19:33
Isaiah 53:9	Buried with the rich	Matthew 27:57–60
Psalms 16:10	Rise from the dead	Matthew 28:9
Psalms 68:18	Ascension	Luke 24:50, 51

My Jewish friend, you have every reason to believe that your Savior has come. Jesus lived, died, rose from the dead, and is coming to earth again. He did this for you. He wants to forgive your sins and come into your life to give purpose and meaning to all that you do.

HOW TO BECOME A "COMPLETE" JEW

- *Repent of your sins.*
  Admit to yourself and God that you have broken His laws and need His mercy.
- *Put your faith in God's Savior—Jesus.*
  Believe that all of God's promises are fulfilled in Messiah Jesus. Trust Him to save you, and Him alone.
- *Receive the Messiah into your heart.*
  Invite Jesus to be your Lord and Savior and to come into your life through His Holy Spirit.

7

Why Do Christians Worship Three Gods?

Moses Maimonides, the famous twelfth-century rabbi, wrote thirteen articles of faith which are a vital part of present-day Jewish liturgy.

There is a daily repeated liturgy of Rabbi Maimonides which reads, "I believe with a perfect faith that the Creator (blessed be His name) is an absolute one."

This statement is the foundation of Judaism. Judaism's greatest text is Deuteronomy 6:4, "Hear, O Israel! The Lord is our God, the Lord is one!"

God is absolute! Jehovah God is one! This is the creed of the Jews, Muslims, Jehovah's Witnesses, even of Hinduism. Then, here come the Christians with their three-headed God: Father, Son, and Holy Spirit! The Trinity—what a mind bender!

Monotheism vs. Polytheism

Do Christians worship three Gods? Is the concept of the Trinity false? These and related questions need to be answered. While professing faith in one God, we as Christians often give the idea to others that we are polytheists.

Our belief in a triune God needs to be explained and thought out. Then Jews, Muslims, and others can truly understand why evangelical Christians believe in only one God.

WHERE DID THE IDEA OF THE TRINITY ORIGINATE?

The word *trinity* is not a biblical word. Its roots are Latin and came to the Church through Tertullian, the great thinker of North Africa. However, the concept of one God in three manifestations is a very definite biblical concept.

Christians did not invent the Trinity. We need to understand that God always has been and always will be a plurality of personalities. He alone is God, and He is changeless in His eternal being.

SOME MISUNDERSTANDINGS ABOUT THE TRINITY

Trinity does not mean tritheism. Christians do not believe in three gods—Father, Son, and Holy Spirit. This is not what *Trinity* implies.

Trinity does not mean God wears different masks to play various parts in the drama of history. Jesus was not a "method" God used. The Holy Spirit is not just the power of God. *Trinity* affirms three distinct persons, yet uniquely one person.

The Unitarian Solution The easy way to avoid this mysterious equation is to make Jesus and the Holy Spirit less than deity. Unitarians, Jehovah's Witnesses, and others have accepted this solution.

DOES SCRIPTURE REVEAL GOD AS THREEFOLD?

We believe God is three in one because the Bible teaches that Jesus of Nazareth was God in the flesh. Also, the Scripture teaches that the Holy Spirit is as much God as the Father and the Son. If we could do away with the idea of Christ as divine and the Holy Spirit as personal, then there would be no argument. Reading the Bible forces us to see God as pluralistic in His oneness.

What does the Bible say about God's personality? This is the real issue. God will be what He has revealed Himself to be in the Scripture. The Scripture is historical evidence of God's nature.

THE OLD TESTAMENT VIEW OF GOD

Is God "plural" in the Old Testament? As we examine some passages, you decide.

Rabbi Maimonides Was Wrong!

Recall Rabbi Maimonides stated in the twelfth century, "I believe, with a perfect faith that the Creator (blessed be His name) is an absolute one."

The Hebrew word that Maimonides used for *absolute* is *Yachid*, meaning "only one"—which is not correct. In Deuteronomy 6:4—which is the *Shema* or decree of Israel's monotheism—Moses (that *other* Moses) calls God *achad*, which means a "united one"—not *yachid*, "only one." Moses calls God a *"united* one," not an *absolute* one. Which Moses are we to believe? Proof that the Hebrew *achad* means *united one* is found in Genesis 2:24, where it says that Adam and Eve became "one [achad] flesh."

Which Moses Is Correct?

Whom do you choose? Moses of the Bible or Moses Maimonides? The Moses of the Bible calls God a "united one" in Judaism's favorite verse, Deuteronomy 6:4. Is this a hint at the Trinity? We Christians believe it is.

There are several other Old Testament passages that indicate the plurality of God's nature:

GENESIS 1:26   "Let *Us* make man in *Our* image . . . ."

GENESIS 3:22   ". . . God said, 'Behold, the man has become like one of *Us* . . . .' "

Here is another allusion to God's nature as plural. God was not talking to angels, because angels cannot create or help God create. He was talking to His Son, the Lord Christ. Colossians 1:15 tells us that Christ created all things. (Read Hebrews 1:2 for reference also.)

Elohim in the Old Testament *El* is Hebrew for God. *Elohim* is the plural: *gods.* Yet often in Genesis, God is called *Elohim.* Rabbis refer to this as a "plural of majesty." It is another indication that God is a "united one"!

The Angel of the Lord In the Old Testament, God often appears to men in different *theophanies,* or God forms (Exodus 16:10). The burning bush of Moses, the *shekinah,* glory in the cloud, or even angellike forms.

Many scholars believe the "angel of the Lord" with whom Jacob wrestled (Genesis 32:24–30) was none other than the preexistent Christ, because Jacob calls the place of his encounter Peniel, which means the face of God. Jacob did not say, "I have seen an angel face-to-face." He knew he had met God and had lived to tell about it!

THE NEW TESTAMENT VIEW OF GOD

Jesus taught us God is three in one.

Matthew 28:19 is the great commission Christ gave His followers. He said, "Go . . . in the name of *the Father, the Son, and the Holy Spirit.*" This was His view of God.

Jesus Claimed Equality With God

John 8:54–59 describes the most dramatic confrontation Jesus ever had with the Jewish leaders of Jerusalem. Here He openly claims deity for Himself in no unmistakable terms that any Jew could understand.

He says, "Your father Abraham rejoiced to see My day; and he saw it, and was glad."

The meaning is clear: Jesus claims to be the Messiah and to have seen Abraham in ages past! The Jews are shocked!

They respond, "You are not even fifty years old, and have You seen Abraham?" Now came the blockbuster! Jesus said to them, "Truly, truly, I say to you, before Abraham was born, I AM."

This language is very strong in English, but it is much stronger in Greek. Literally translated, Jesus said, "Before Abraham came into being, I myself continually existed." The words *I am* are a deliberate allusion to Exodus 3:14, where God speaks His name to Moses. God says, "I AM WHO I AM." This wording comes from the Hebrew verb *hayah,*"to be." Jesus' words "I am" come from the Greek verb *to be.* Astonishing! Jesus is claiming to be the Lord God Yahweh who spoke to Moses!

Make no mistake about it, the Jews got His message. They took up stones to kill Him!

Chapter 17 of John is Christ's prayer for His followers. In verse 5 it is recorded that Jesus says, "And now, glorify Thou Me together with Thyself, Father, with the glory which I ever had with Thee before the world was."

It is evident again that Jesus is claiming equality with God in His preincarnate state.

The Apostle Paul's Doctrine of God

In 2 Corinthians 13:14 we read, "The grace of the Lord Jesus Christ, and the love of God, and the fellowship of the Holy Spirit, be with you all."

Here Paul gives the blessing of God as a benediction to this letter. This God is threefold in the mind of Paul. Notice the words: *"fellowship* of the Holy Spirit." The Holy Spirit is a person, not an "it," or some abstract force emanating from godlike cosmic electricity. (For a further look at Paul's understanding of the Trinity, see 1 Corinthians 12:4–6; 2 Corinthians 13:14; Philippians 2:6–8; and Titus 2:13.)

The Witness of Peter to the Trinity

First Peter 1:2 states, ". . . according to the foreknowledge of God the Father, by the sanctifying work of the Spirit, that you may obey Jesus Christ and be sprinkled with His blood . . . ."

It is again asserted that God is threefold. So you see the New Testament picks up where the Old Testament began. God is a united one.

EXPLAINING THE TRINITY TO OTHERS

The God of the Scriptures Is a Revealed God

Regardless of our preconceived ideas about who and what God is, we must limit our theology to what God has shown Himself to be in and through the Judaic-Christian Scriptures. Therefore, because of the divinity of Jesus Christ and the personality of the Spirit, we must make a sensible statement of the Trinity.

Some Practical Aids in Presenting the Trinity

Avoid using meaningless, impersonal metaphors to explain God as threefold. For example, I've heard people say, "The Trinity is like the stages of water, ice, and steam." However, water can't be ice and steam and water at the same time!

Therefore, it is helpful to illustrate the Trinity in personal terms. For example, my name is Barry Wood. I am a father to my children, a son to my father, a husband to my wife, and a teacher to my students. How can I be both a father and a son? Obviously my personality is pluralistic and can handle each relationship respectively. Who I am and how I function (as husband, father, son, teacher) depends upon the need at any given moment.

So it is with God. As the Father, He relates Himself to creation as its Creator and Sustainer. As the Son, He relates Himself to man's need of forgiveness and redemption. As the Holy Spirit, He personalizes His presence to men to convict of sin, to encourage the heart. His personality is as functional as is yours.

The Great Hang-Up

Now here comes our problem: We always tend to describe the Trinity of God in terms of the historical life of the man Jesus of Nazareth. This is indeed unfortunate. The Trinity should not be discussed in the nonnormative terms of the Incarnation.

The Incarnation was an abnormal period in the experience of God. The thirty years the Messiah was on earth in the flesh was *not* God's normal relationship to Himself or to the universe. God has always been Father (love), Son (saving grace), and Holy Spirit (abiding presence). Yet, God as Son has not always had a flesh-and-bone body. God's normal "form" is spirit. God is a spirit being. Because of man's sin and need of salvation, God's love had to embody itself in the Messiah ("a Son," as Psalms 2:7 says). The name we give to God as Savior is *Jesus*. His name means deliverer, or savior. This historical manifestation of God's heart was only temporary. The "infleshing" of God was an abnormal experience for God. (*See* John 1:14: God has always been Savior; He has not always been Savior in a physical Jewish body!).

What Happened to the Body?

At the Ascension (*see* Acts 1:9, 10) Jesus was bodily lifted up into the heavens out of the sight of the disciples. Does He still have a body? I don't think so, because the Scripture nowhere states that He does.

It seems to me that God has had three body forms in history:

God in Spirit Form: John 4:24 Spirit does have form. In eternity past, God as Father, Son, and Holy Spirit, was all in one form. God as spirit was a united one.

God in Human Form: Philippians 2:7 For thirty years God had two forms. As Father, He was spirit God; as Savior, He was in flesh. Jesus was the God/man.

God in Spirit-Body Form: John 20:26 The Resurrection body of Jesus was a spirit-body form. It could be seen, yet was not flesh and bone. (By "flesh and bone" we mean a normal human body. Jesus during his Resurrection appearances challenged Thomas to touch Him, although it is not stated that he actually did so. Also He ate with the disciples on the shore of Galilee during the Resurrection period. His body was real, but was capable of appearing and disappearing.) This body was temporary. It was accommodative to our human senses as proof that Jesus was indeed raised from the dead.

Now, what happened to His spirit body at the Ascension? It was changed, just as the flesh-and-bone body in the tomb was changed. Jesus, as God, has no distinct separate body now. He is God in God's prehistorical form. "Absorbed," as it were, back into the Godhead.

Therefore, when we Christians pray to God we are not praying to three persons. I don't see God as an old man with a beard sitting on a throne with Jesus His Son sitting on His right and the Holy Spirit sitting on the left. NO! This is not the Trinity.

The God Who Acts

We believe in the God of history. He has shown Himself to be a "united one." *This* is the God we love and serve.

8

Jesus and Muhammad

Perhaps one-seventh of the world's population, approximately five hundred million people, are Muslims. Both spellings—*Muslim* and *Moslem*—are correct. The first is the actual Arabic word; the second simply transliterates the Arabic vowel sound for *us* into *o*. The *s* is sounded *ss*, not *z*.

In America alone there are 150,000 Muslims, and that does not include international students and others on temporary visas. This figure also excludes the Black Muslims, whom orthodox Muslims consider heretics. Muhammad and his people have left the land of the crescent and moved west.

The Oil Crisis Since 1973 and the oil crisis, the Arabs are now the center of attention in the world's financial arena. Millions of dollars in Muslim money are being spent in America. Muhammad is buying up Boardwalk and Park Place in America's Monopoly game. The Arabs are here to stay.

East Meets West Because of the great influx of Middle East culture into the American scene, it is imperative that the Christian meet his new "neighbor." This became literally true for me a couple of years ago in Los Angeles when a Muslim family from Pakistan moved in next door to us. That's when I began to brush up on Islamic belief. (The word Islam [iss-lahm'] comes from an Arabic word of three consonants, *S L M*. Its primary meaning is to escape from danger.

My purpose in writing this chapter is twofold. First, to give some brief background on Islam to help us learn about Muhammad and the religion he founded. Second, to present some ideas on how the Christian can share Christ with the Muslim.

Who Is Muhammad? According to Muslims, the greatest of all the prophets and the founder of their religion was Muhammad. Born in Mecca in A.D. 570, Muhammad was orphaned at age six and was raised as a humble shepherd boy under the watchcare of his uncle. For a detailed biography of Muhammad the prophet, see *The Religion of Islam* by Ahmad A. Galwash (Hefner Publishing Co., New York).

As he grew up, he became a skilled camel driver and often helped with the caravans of his uncle. He rose to the position of manager of the camel caravans and eventually married a wealthy Meccan widow named Khadija. Although Khadija was fifteen years his senior, they were happily married for twenty-five years.

For fifteen years he lived quietly managing his wife's estate, working with his hands, and generally living the life of a peasant.

Gabriel Calls Outside of Mecca there was a cave on Mount Hira where Muhammad often retreated for solitary contemplation and prayer. One evening while he was visiting this cave a storm came up, and out of the storm Muhammad says he heard a loud voice telling him to "Read." The uneducated camel driver protested that he could not read, only to hear the voice command him again to read. In desperation he asked, "What can I read?" He was shown a scroll on which words were emblazoned with fire. Muhammad testifies that miraculously he read the scroll, even though he had never before read a word. Later, the voice gone, the words were still vividly burned upon his memory.

As Muhammad was to tell the story, he left the cave, fearing he had gone mad or was possessed. To his astonishment, however, he again heard the voice from heaven. This time the voice identified itself. Looking up, he saw the angel Gabriel in human form saying to him, "O Muhammad! You are Allah's messenger, and I am Gabriel."

Muhammad testifies that this dramatic calling was not enough to convince him. Some time later another divine call was issued. While in deep meditation and agony of soul, he felt himself called again by a voice from heaven. "Arise and warn," it commanded, "and thy Lord do thou magnify!"

It was at this point that Muhammad yielded himself totally to the will of Allah. He became the apostle of God, never to waiver again. His main mission in life was to proclaim a pure monotheism to his idolatrous people.

Years of Persecution His views were not readily accepted. Only members of his immediate family believed him at first. When he stood before his tribe to preach his beliefs in the one true God and condemned their idolatry, he met with great resistance. What followed was more than ten years of persecution and exile. Meccans were very hostile to Muhammad's claims to be God's apostle. Some believed; most did not.

More Revelations As time passed, Muhammad claimed more revelations were given him by Allah. He proclaimed himself to be the successor to the great prophets—Noah, Abraham, Moses, Jesus, and others. Eventually he saw himself as the final messenger God would ever send to the world. He was *the* prophet! It was now only a matter of time before this disciplined, dedicated leader would conquer Arabia with his doctrine.

To Medina In A.D. 622, a group of some 150 Muslims secretly left Mecca to go to the town of Yathrib. Later that fall, Muhammad came to Yathrib, escorted by 70 warriors.

The day Muhammad entered Yathrib is a holy day for Muslims. The Muslim calendar begins on this date of September 20, A.D. 622. Yathrib was renamed Medina in honor of the Prophet's eight-year residence there.

Conquest of Mecca At the age of 60, Muhammad and his army marched into Mecca to claim it as the holy city of Islam. Against unbelievable odds, the Prophet had won victory after victory until at last even Mecca had been subdued. Then two years later, Muhammad died.

Religion by Conquest Muhammad had set a pattern for his followers. The will of Allah must be done. His enemies must be destroyed. Almost immediately Islam spread beyond the borders of Arabia. By 636, Jerusalem was captured, and by 715 the Arab empire had spread from the Chinese frontier westward to the Atlantic Ocean. Islam today ranks as a religious influence and is a power to be reckoned with in the world economy. So with this brief history behind us, what then does Islam teach?

WHAT DOES ISLAM BELIEVE?

Islam believes the Quran. Indeed, Islam *is* the Quran. This book, divided into 114 chapters (called *suras*), is the Bible to the Muslim world. It contains the words and revelations given to Muhammad. Although he did not write the Quran, his followers wrote these sayings down shortly after his death. Muslims believe every written word is just as God spoke it to the Prophet.

The Quran and the Bible

The Quran holds a place of divine worship to the Muslim. It is infallible. God spoke His last word to the world through His last prophet, Muhammad. The Quran states that the Jewish-Christian Scriptures are divinely inspired also, but that they have been repeatedly falsified by Jews

and Christians, so that whenever the Quran and the Bible
conflict, only the Quran can be trusted.

What this means is that Muhammad is the sole interpreter
of Scripture! He alone knows the truth about Abraham,
Moses, Jesus, and the prophets. Quite often you'll find that
the Quran tells a very different story from what the Christian is used to hearing. For example, the narratives of Jesus'
birth and His crucifixion are so different in the Quran that
one asks, "Who is that?" But, to the Moslem, the Quran is
always right. It is the final authority. (See sura 33:40.)

The Islamic Creed

Islam demands absolute acceptance of and faith in six
basic beliefs. These basic doctrines are sometimes called
the Islamic creed. These teachings are all found throughout
the Quran.

The Unity of God   Islam's favorite creed is "There is no
God but God." This creed is daily recited by the faithful
Muslim. Islam abhors the idea that God has any "as-
sociates," and therefore has great difficulty understanding
the concept of the Trinity. The Quran says in sura 5:76:

> They do blaspheme who say
> God is one of three
> In a Trinity; for there is
> No god but God.

As we shall learn later, Muhammad didn't have a clear
understanding of the Trinity, and we as Christians must
show the Muslims that we do not worship three Gods or the
Virgin Mary.

The Quran presents God as very remote and almost un-
definable. He is not the personal God of the Bible who can
be personally experienced. He is a God to be absolutely
obeyed, not known or loved.

There are ninety-nine names for God in the Quran. He is

called All-Knowing, Merciful, Sovereign, Holy One, Guardian of the Faith, Exalted, and Supreme, to list a few. The Christian notices that two names are missing from the list. God is never called Love or Father. In fact, the idea of God as a Father is considered blasphemous. The Quran says:

> They say: The Most Gracious
> Has begotten a son!
> Indeed ye have put forth
> A thing most monstrous!
> For it is not compatible
> with the majesty of God that He
> should beget a son.
> Jesus Christ the son of Mary,
> was no more than an apostle of God.
>   Sura 19:88–89, 92

When we come to talk about sharing Christ with Muslims we will discuss the concept of God as a Father and Jesus as the Son of God.

The Doctrine of Angels   Muslims make much of their belief in angels. Through the angel Gabriel came the Quran to Muhammad. Angels are God's messengers. One will find little difference between the biblical concept of angels and that of Islam.

Satan is believed to be a fallen angel and has other fallen angels who serve him.

It is important to understand that God is so remote from man that He doesn't deal with man directly. He uses His angels and prophets as His envoys. This is why it is so hard for the Muslim to understand that God could become a man in Jesus Christ.

The Sacred Books   The third basic tenet of Islam is the belief that God has revealed His will through scripture. Muslim scripture includes:

- The Old Testament (particularly the first five books)
- The Gospels (which have been "lost" and are there-
  fore not accurate, since the Gospels do not agree
  among themselves).
- The Quran
- The Traditions, called the *Hadith*

The Hadith contains traditional sayings and actions of
Muhammad that are *not* in the Quran. The Hadith serves as
a commentary on the Quran.

Of these sacred books, only the Quran is totally trustworthy as God's pure word.

The Prophets It is stated that there are 125,000 prophets
who have existed as God's special messengers. The Quran
mentions only 25 prophets. The principal prophets are
Abraham, Moses, Jesus, and Muhammad. Muhammad is
the last and greatest of the prophets. Because Muhammad
was sent to all mankind (rather than just to the Jews), he
supersedes all others.

Muslims believe Jesus was only a prophet sent to the
Jews. He was not the Son of God. He did not die for the sins
of the world. The Quran teaches that Jesus will return to
earth at the end of the age to be judged along with all other
men.

The Day of Judgment Islam is very eschatological.
Muhammad put great emphasis upon the coming Day of
Judgment. Allah's day of wrath is coming. There will be a
payday someday.

- All men will be judged according to their works.
- All Muslims will enter paradise, though some will be
  purged for their sins first.
- Non-Muslims will be condemned eternally.
- There is a paradise and a hell (pit of fire).

Predestination There can be no understanding of Islam's idea of God without realizing that God is not so much

a person as He is absolute deity, an indescribable God whose will is law. Allah is to be obeyed. The goal of religion for the Muslim is to *obey* God, not to get to *know* God. He is not knowable!

This then is the Islamic creed.

WHERE DOES ISLAM DIFFER FROM CHRISTIANITY?

It has been said that all world religions are basically the same and therefore it doesn't make any difference what you believe. An international student from Jordan said to me, "You Christians worship the same God I do. I just call Him Allah and you call Him Jehovah." Was he correct? Are the differences worth mentioning? I'm afraid that this Jordanian student was too naive. There are some very marked differences between Jesus and Muhammad. The Christian witness needs to be aware of these in order to adequately share his faith.

The Question of Biblical Authority

Muhammad has claimed infallibility for his revelations as God's prophet. The Quran is the censor of all other scripture. Yet the Bible stands the test of time as a true historical record. The Muslim must be led to see that the Bible has not been falsified and distorted. What right has Muhammad to assert that his revelations are correct and the Gospels are wrong? What evidence is there that the Scriptures are incorrect just because the Quran disagrees? The Christian witness should challenge the Muslim to prove the Bible has been tampered with. (See chapter 1, "Can We Trust the Bible?")

The Quran and Jesus

Most Muslims take the Quran as their source of information about Jesus and the early Church. The Muslim has been told that the true gospel of Jesus has been "lost." Therefore, he believes what he reads about Jesus in the Quran is the whole truth. And yet, the Jesus of the Quran is not the Jesus of the Gospels. They are two different people. Someone is wrong. It is necessary to challenge the Muslim to read for himself the Gospel record. He needs to know that all knowledgeable scholarship regards the Gospel documents as reliable. Now my question is, who is a better source to write a biography of Jesus of Nazareth—someone who was an eyewitness (such as John the Apostle) or someone who lived 600 years later (like Muhammad)? If the Gospels are not a historical documentary on Jesus of Nazareth, then there *is* no reliable history anywhere.

The Virgin Birth

The Quran	*The Bible*
States that Jesus was born of a virgin but was not the Son of God. He was created by God from clay as was Adam. (Sura 4:177 and 3:59.)	"And the angel said to her, 'Do not be afraid, Mary; for you have found favor with God. And behold you will conceive in your womb, and bear a son, and you shall name Him Jesus'" (Luke 1:30, 31).
	"And the angel answered and said to her, 'The Holy Spirit will come upon you, and the power of the Most High will overshadow you; and for that reason the holy offspring shall be called the Son of God'" (Luke 1:35).

The Person of Christ

The Quran

Jesus Christ, the son of Mary, was no more than an apostle of God. (Sura 19:92.)

The Quran says Jesus is only a prophet to the Jews. Muhammad is the prophet to the whole world.

The Bible

"And Simon Peter answered and said, 'Thou art the Christ, the Son of the living God' " (Matthew 16:16).

"And He is the radiance of His glory and the exact representation of His nature, and upholds all things by the word of His power. When He had made purification of sins, He sat down at the right hand of the Majesty on high" (Hebrews 1:3).

The Cross of Christ

The Quran

Speaking of the crucifixion it says, "They neither killed nor crucified him; it had only the appearance of it" (sura 4:157, 158).

Islam is docetic in its idea of the crucifixion. *Docetic* (from the Greek *dokëo*, meaning to appear, to seem) refers to the idea that it only "seemed" that Jesus died.

The Bible

"But He was pierced through for our transgressions, He was crushed for our iniquities; The chastening for our well-being fell upon Him, And by His scourging we are healed. All of us like sheep have gone astray, Each of us has turned to his own way; But the Lord has caused the iniquity of us all to fall on Him" (Isaiah 53:5, 6).

The Bible

"From that time Jesus
Christ began to show His
disciples that He must go to
Jerusalem, and suffer many
things from the elders and
chief priests and scribes,
and be killed, and be raised
up on the third day"
(Matthew 16:21).

". . . having cancelled out
the certificate of debt con-
sisting of decrees against us
and which was hostile to us;
and He has taken it out of
the way, having nailed it to
the cross. When He had dis-
armed the rulers and au-
thorities, He made a public
display of them, having
triumphed over them
through Him" (Colossians
2:14, 15).

The New Testament writers, all of whom were eyewit-
nesses to the historical death, burial, and Resurrection of
Jesus Christ, affirm that Jesus' death was real and that it was
planned of God that He should die for the sins of the world.
If the Quran is indeed correct that another man died in
Jesus' place, then:

- The apostles are all liars. If they lied about Jesus'
  death and Resurrection, then how do we know they
  told the truth about His life?
- Allah is unjust to make an innocent man die for something Jesus did.

- The testimony of the early Church weighs heavily against the witness of Muhammad as to the crucifixion of Jesus Christ.
- The cross is not where a prophet met defeat, as the Quran would see Christ's death, but rather the cross is where God defeated Satan and forgives sin for all mankind. (*See* 1 Peter 3:18, 19.)

The Return of Christ

The Quran	*The Bible*
Teaches that Jesus will return at the end of the age to be judged with the rest of humanity and then die. (Sura 3.)	Christ returns as the Judge of heaven and earth to establish His Kingdom. (*See* Revelation 19:11–16.)

The Quran and the Trinity

Islam is monotheistic. Any major confusion between Muhammad and Christianity comes at the point of Muhammad's understanding of the biblical doctrine of the Trinity. The Quran condemns the idea of the Trinity as blasphemous. Here are some samples of Muhammad's statements about the Trinity:

Say not three: God is one only divinity (sura 4:169).

They surely are infidels who say God is the third of three (sura 5:177).

O Jesus, son of Mary, has thou said unto mankind, "Take me and my mother as two Gods beside God?" (Sura 5:116).

Did Muhammad Reject the Trinity? If these verses are representative (as they are) of the Quran's teaching on the

Trinity, it is very obvious to the average Christian that Muhammad did not understand the Trinity! Any evangelical Christian would agree wholeheartedly with the above verses. If anyone says God is three, or is the third of three, or that the Virgin Mary is deity, then he is a heretic from the historic Christian faith. Yet it seems that Muhammad thought that is what we Christians believe. The idea that God is three persons and three substances is the second-century heresy of modalism, which said that God has appeared in three "modes." This heresy denied the deity of Christ and was rejected by the early Church. So you see the Quran does not repudiate Christian teaching on the Trinity, because the Quran never states our belief nor does it understand it.

Christianity Is Monotheistic   In witnessing to the Muslim we must help him understand that the early Christians were Jews. These Jewish believers in Jesus were monotheists. Muhammad did not invent the oneness of God—Moses beat him to it by nearly two thousand years.

We Christians do not believe in the Father, Son, and Mary. Nor is the Trinity a belief in three Gods. We believe in one God who has revealed His nature to man three ways. See chapter 7, "Why Do Christians Worship Three Gods?"

The Quran and Salvation

Now we come to a most important doctrinal question. How does a man go to heaven (paradise) and how are sins forgiven? On many Muslim buildings there is a representation of a pair of scales, or balances. These balances convey the idea of divine justice. They remind the faithful of the way of salvation in the Quran.

The Quran	*The Bible*
"They whose balances shall be heavy shall be blest. But	"He saved us, not on the basis of deeds which we

The Quran

they whose balances shall be light, they shall lose their soul, abiding in hell forever" (sura 13:102–104).

The Bible

have done in righteousness, but according to His mercy, by the washing of regeneration and renewing by the Holy Spirit" (Titus 3:5).

"For by grace you have been saved through faith; and that not of yourselves, it is the gift of God; not as a result of works, that no one should boast" (Ephesians 2:8, 9).

"Now we know that whatever the Law says, it speaks to those who are under the Law, that every mouth may be closed, and all the world may become accountable to God; because by the works of the Law no flesh will be justified in His sight; for through the Law comes the knowledge of sin. But now apart from the Law the righteousness of God has been manifested, being witnessed by the Law and the Prophets; even the righteousness of God through faith in Jesus Christ for all those who believe; for there is no distinction" (Romans 3:19–22).

The Bible

> "Jesus said to him, 'I am the
> way, and the truth, and the
> life; no one comes to the
> Father, but through Me' "
> (John 14:6).

Islam is absolute obedience to the will of Allah. There is
no assurance of forgiveness in the Quran. How many good
works does it take to please Allah and make the balance tip
in your favor? Allah does not say. The Quran teaches that
most Muslims will have to undergo purging in the afterlife.

What Is Sin?   The Quran has no concept of original sin
and the need of redemption. Because God is remote and
impersonal there is no real motivation to please Him, nor is
there power within to live according to His will.

To the Muslim, sin is only forgetfulness. It is forgetting to
do the will of Allah. In the Bible, sin is a disposition toward
rebellion in the human heart. Man needs a new heart, a
new birth. Only the sinless life of God's Son, Jesus, can
forgive sin. Salvation comes only through the shed blood of
the Messiah—Jesus Christ. Jesus claimed He was the only
way to the Father.

Salvation Is a Relationship With God   Here is the great
difference between Islam and Christianity: Islam offers
servitude to God; Jesus Christ offers sonship with God.
Salvation to the Christian is a personal fellowship with the
Living God.

PRINCIPLES IN WITNESSING TO A MUSLIM

Assuming we have digested much of the background of
Islam and have a working knowledge of what the Muslim
believes, we are now ready to share with him our faith that
Jesus Christ is the Savior of the world. Here are some principles and procedures for sharing:

Avoid belittling the Muslim's religion. Because of his intense faith in the credibility of the Quran, the Muslim will be very defensive and argumentative. Our motive is love. We must outlove and outlive the Muslim. Show him Christ lives by letting Christ love and live through you. Never argue with anyone about religion—*period!*

Begin by identifying with Islam's monotheism. Show the Muslim Deuteronomy 6:4. Help him understand that the Christian believes in only one God. Avoid the idea of Trinity at first, but be prepared to share the threefoldness of God if necessary.

Share with him the many things that Islam has in common with Christianity:

> Belief in one God
> Need for a moral life
> Eternal reward and punishment

Center your conversation on the person and work of Jesus Christ. Contrast Muhammad as the Prophet and Jesus as the Son of God.

Share the true meaning of the virgin birth (which the Quran believes in). Use John 1:1, 14, 18; Hebrews 1:3; Philippians 2:6–11.

Share why Jesus came into the world: He came to save us from sin (Luke 19:10); He is the sinless Son of God (Isaiah 9:6).

Explain the cross as God's victory over evil (Colossians 2:14, 15).

Share that, in Jesus, God reveals Himself as a loving Father. In Islam, revelation is *from* God; in Jesus, revelation is *of* God. Jesus reveals God's heart toward us as "Father."

Stress that salvation by grace produces a holy life through the indwelling Holy Spirit. Tell him he can know God personally and have assurance of eternal life.

9

Why Does God Allow Evil and Suffering?

Perhaps you've asked the questions, "Why would a good God create such an evil world? Why would He (if He exists) allow babies to be born deformed, or cancer to plague the lives of thousands?" The questions are real and cry out for answers, especially if you've been touched by pain or evil in a personal way. It's hard enough to believe in God, but it's even harder to believe when life tumbles in on you!

SOME FACTORS WHICH RAISE QUESTIONS ABOUT EVIL

The Bible declares:

- That God is good ("Our Father, who art in heaven . . ." [Matthew 6:9])
- That God is all-powerful ("Holy, Holy, Holy, is the Lord God, the Almighty . . ." [Revelation 4:8])
- That evil is real ("Put on the full armor of God, that you may be able to stand firm against the schemes of the devil" [Ephesians 6:11]).

These three statements create our three-pronged problem: If God were good, He would wish to make His creatures perfectly happy. If He were almighty, He would certainly be able to make them happy. His creatures are not happy; therefore, God lacks either goodness, power, or both.

SOME WRONG ANSWERS TO THIS ETHICAL PUZZLE

There have been some unsatisfactory attempts to resolve this dilemma by eliminating one of the three realities:

Dualism

This philosophy says there are two ultimate realities: a good god and an evil god. It is the answer of the popular Persian religion, Zoroastrianism, which has two gods who are continually at war with each other.

Christian Dualism Some misguided Christians get caught in this kind of false theology by making the devil a second god. The devil exists, but he is a created being (a fallen angel [Ezekiel 28:13–16]) and not equal to God. He is not all-powerful.

Puritanism This has said by its philosophy that God is good but the world is evil. Therefore God has nothing to do with the world or its systems. The result was that puritan theology preached only "pie in the sky by and by," with no concern for this world. This too is to dodge the issue.

A Finite, Limited God

Several years ago E. S. Brightman wrote a book entitled *The Finite God* in which he offers the solution that God wants to help us with our suffering, but cannot, because He is not all-powerful.

Brightman says God cares when we suffer but He can't always help. He suffers when we suffer. For example, when I get a toothache, Brightman says, God gets a cosmic toothache.

Evil Is Not Real

Here is the third unsatisfactory attempt to solve the problem by removing the reality of evil. If evil isn't real, then we have no problem.

Eastern religions have taken this position. Hinduism (the mother of most Eastern thought) says evil is only a passing appearance; it has no real essence—like heat from fire. Everything in this world is *maya,* or illusion. Evil is merely the absence of good; it is not a real thing in itself (a kind of reasoning that rejects the biblical doctrine of Satan, et cetera).

Christian Science is an Americanized version of this solution. Christian Science seems to be saying you have no real pain; it's all in your mind.

All of these solutions are unsatisfactory, because they seek to eliminate one or more of the realities of life. A good God does exist, evil is real, and the world is a mess. Why? Let's find a way to cope with these realities.

HOW TO SOLVE THE PROBLEM
OF EVIL AND SUFFERING

First, we must distinguish between moral evil and natural evil:

Moral Evil

Some evil is caused by moral agents, human or demonic, and affects even the innocent.

Example: Many of the children in orphanages are there because of the abuse of alcohol. God cannot be blamed for orphans or for creating the chemicals from which alcohol is made. The fault lies with the parent who drinks it.

Example: A baby is born deformed because of the mother's drug abuse, or a baby is born blind because of the mother's venereal disease. Is God to blame, or is the mother's sin to blame?

Natural Evil

Some evil is the result of natural phenomena such as snakebite, tornadoes, and hurricanes. The snake is not evil in itself. It can become evil when it bites you and causes pain and suffering.

A second thing we must do is to look at suffering and evil from different perspectives:

The Teaching Principle

We learn from life's experiences. God teaches us through the good and the bad.

Romans 5:3, 4 says,"We can rejoice, too, when we run into problems and trials for we know that they are good for us—they help us learn to be patient" (LB).

Example: A child burns his hand, and so learns to respect fire.

The Eschatological View

Things will work out in the end. Often we don't understand why something happens to us at the moment it happens, but in the end God will work out His purpose through it.

Example: The exile of the Jews in Babylon was used of God to create hope and faith in their restoration. Much Old Testament literature was written as a result of the exile. Romans 8:28 states this principle: "And we know that God causes all things to work together for good to those who love God . . . ."

Evil Is a Mystery

This is the teaching of the Book of Job. Why did God allow Job to be tested? Some have philosophized on the subject but the book itself gives no answer. Some things that happen just must be left unanswered until God chooses to reveal their purpose. God says, "For My thoughts are not your thoughts, Neither are your ways My ways . . ." (Isaiah 55:8).

Evil Is Relative

Some have said that evil and suffering are only matters of interpretation. They say nothing is evil in itself.

Example: A tornado is not intrinsically evil, neither is a spider or a rattlesnake. Only when they affect us are they interpreted as evil. Of course there is an element of truth in this idea.

Suffering Is Vicarious

Evil can have a vicarious result. Men die in behalf of others, and good comes from it. War is evidence of this. Also, the vicarious death of Jesus is an example. However, neither war nor the death of Jesus would have happened were men not sinners.

Evil Is Punitive

Evil is for punishment, and we have only ourselves to blame. This position is stated in Galatians 6:7: "Do not be deceived, God is not mocked; for whatever a man sows, this he will also reap."

There is truth in all of these explanations, but none is sufficient in itself. Each individual must interpret life's circumstances for himself. No one can tell another person *why* suffering has come. This is graphically illustrated by Job's well-meaning friends.

You and I must learn to translate the question from, Why did it happen? to What does this mean in the light of my relationship to God? You and I don't have to know *why*, but, we do need to know God cares and that He is personally related to every experience in life. We are not to be prespeculative, but rather postspeculative: Time or eternity will tell us why God allowed the suffering.

GOD HIMSELF IS INVOLVED IN YOUR HURTS

Calvary's cross is historical evidence of God's very real involvement in our suffering:

> He was despised and forsaken of men, A man of sorrows, and acquainted with grief; And like one from whom men hide their face, He was despised, and we did not esteem Him. Surely our griefs He Himself bore, And our sorrows He carried; Yet we ourselves esteemed Him stricken, Smitten of God, and afflicted. But He was pierced through for our transgressions, He was crushed for our iniquities; The chastening for our well-being fell upon Him, And by His scourging we are healed.
>
> Isaiah 53:3–5

Because of evil and suffering, God gave His Son Jesus. The cross says to you and me that God is going to defeat evil and He is going to overcome evil with good. His Kingdom is coming. You need to believe God is good and let your hurts and sorrows drive you to Him for salvation and comfort. Listen to the words of Paul:

> Blessed be the God and Father of our Lord Jesus Christ, the Father of mercies and God of all comfort; who comforts us in all our affliction so that we may be able to comfort those who are in any affliction with the comfort with which we ourselves are comforted by God. For just as the sufferings of Christ are ours in abundance, so also our comfort is abundant through Christ.
>
> 2 Corinthians 1:3–5

10

What About Children Who Die?

Do children who die go to heaven? What about the place called limbo—and original sin? These questions are often asked by unbelievers or those who have heard some teaching from Roman Catholics.

A woman I was trying to lead to Christ had recently been to a church where a baby was sprinkled. This ceremony raised questions in her mind. She said, "Well, if that sweet little baby had to be baptized to keep God from sending it to hell, then I want no part of that kind of God!"

Some Vital Questions

When we consider the subject of children and infant baptism there are some questions that need answering.

- Are babies born with the guilt of original sin?
- Are babies and children damned without baptism?
- When does a child become morally accountable to God?
- What is original sin anyway?

These questions need biblical answers, because many a parent has lost a child to death and has questioned the goodness of God. We must determine what the Bible says about children.

THE OLD TESTAMENT AND CHILDREN

As we examine the Old Testament we discover that the Scriptures are strangely silent on the subject. The Old Testament addresses itself to adults and has very little to say about the spiritual status of children. However, this silence may be a clue. If Moses wasn't worried about them, then he must have had a reason.

The Sons of the Covenant

Israel was taught that children are a part of the covenant family of Israel. They along with their parents are God's chosen people. A child was thus under the protection of Jehovah God. This was symbolized in the circumcision of male infants when eight days old.

Then, as the sons grew to manhood and were ready to understand and participate in the religion of Israel, they were initiated into the faith by means of Bar Mitzvah at approximately the age of twelve. At this time the child could choose for himself whether he believed in God or not. (The concept of the Sons of the Covenant covered female children as well, but the female is not mentioned because lineage was through the male.)

The Age of Accountability

From this Old Testament tradition has come the idea that all children are under the protection of God's grace until they come to the "age of accountability." This term simply means that a child will eventually come to the age where he has a moral consciousness of right and wrong and can comprehend how to receive Christ as Savior. The chronological age will vary from child to child depending upon the religious training he receives (or lack of it!).

THE NEW TESTAMENT AND CHILDREN

Here again we face a silence on the issue. Neither Jesus nor the apostles give us direct discourse on the status of children. Jesus said, "Permit the children to come to me, and do not hinder them, for the kingdom of heaven belongs to such as these" (*see* Matthew 19:14). Again He said, "Unless you are converted and become like children, you shall not enter the kingdom of heaven" (Matthew 18:3). These statements are about the only clues we have as to the status of children before God. Yet the silence of Scripture strongly testifies that children are "innocent until proven guilty" as far as God is concerned.

Why all the fuss then? Because a nonbiblical tradition has confused us. Somewhere the idea arose that a baby is contaminated by his parents' "original sin," as though sin were transmitted genetically or were hereditary.

The Second-Century Gnostics

How is sin transmitted? The Bible doesn't tell us. Yet, some early Church theologians tried to! Among them were the Greek Gnostics, whose background in Greek philosophy brought several false teachings into the Church in the first through fourth centuries. It was common teaching among the Gnostics that sin is a "physical" reality. Gnosticism held that "all flesh is evil," supposing that sin was embedded somehow in our flesh. Therefore, it is passed down to children like a disease—or so the argument ran. This incorrect reasoning reached doctrinal status under St. Augustine in the latter part of the fourth century.

Augustine and Original Sin

Augustine was a bishop in North Africa. He was influenced by this Gnostic idea that sin is a "physical" reality. In discussing Paul's teaching in Romans 5:12–21 regarding original sin, Augustine said that sin was transmitted from parent to child in what he called, "seminal propagation." I think Augustine erred when he saw sin as a physical thing rather than an attitude. From his teaching about original sin came the conclusion that babies carry the guilt of their parents' sin; therefore, a baby must be cleansed. The next step for the Roman Church was to find a "means of grace" that would forgive and remove this guilt. Infant baptism was the answer! It is not a biblical answer, but it became the Roman solution.

What Is Original Sin?

In Romans 5:12 Paul writes, "Therefore, just as through one man sin entered into the world, and death through sin, and so death spread to all men, because all sinned."

Now, if this is a statement of original sin, what does it tell us?

- Adam's sin was the source of all human sin.
- The result of Adam's rebellion was "death through sin." Both physical and spiritual death are the result of the fall of Adam.
- A further result is that "death spread to all men." Here is where the misunderstanding comes. Notice *death* spread to all men, not guilt or damnation. This death means that all men since Adam have "death" in them: We are dead to God, spiritually dead. This spiritual deadness makes it inevitable that we will one day willfully rebel against God. It is our nature to do so.
- Then the fourth phrase Paul uses is very meaningful: "because all sinned." Here comes the guilt. We are not accountable until we sin. We are not guilty because Adam sinned but because we ourselves sin. Thus a child is born with a spiritual deadness which

shows itself as a selfish tendency toward self-centeredness. Somewhere in that child's maturation he will intentionally sin. At that moment he becomes guilty, not before. Because of this inborn proclivity toward self, there never has been, nor will there ever be, a "son of Adam" who will not sin.

CHILDREN ARE UNDER THE WATCHCARE OF JESUS

What then are we to conclude? The issue was stated clearly by Dr. William Hendricks, professor of theology, Southwestern Baptist Theological Seminary, Fort Worth, in a class lecture in systematic theology:

> It is reasonable to assume, that since the Biblical record does not speak specifically about how sin is transmitted, nor does it indicate the status of children incapable of response, and since they do reflect the confirmation of the sons of the covenant and are addressed to persons capable of making a response; then children are under the grace of God. Also, we are to assume that sin and condemnation imply something of personal participation.

Children are innocent until they individually respond to God in rebellion. This statement would imply that children or the mentally retarded are not accountable. Only God knows when a person is ready for the gospel. Some retarded persons never come to the age of accountability and are under God's watchcare, just like a little child. It is my understanding that children who die go immediately to be with the Lord, perhaps escorted by guardian angels (*see* Matthew 18:10) into the presence of God.

When Does One Become Accountable?

At what point is anyone, child or adult, accountable for his sins?

When We Know What Sin Is It is the parent's and the Church's role to teach us about God and His attitude toward sin. When we understand that sin is against God, this is the first step toward salvation.

When We Understand Atonement At some point we must comprehend the significance of the cross. Jesus died for my sins. His death was for me. Each person must come to terms with the substitutionary death of Jesus Christ.

We Must Understand What It Means to Be Lost Once we come to terms with our own sins and realize that God sent His only Son to forgive us, then the Spirit of God can reveal to us our lost condition. When any person, child or adult, comes to this place in his life, he is ready to be saved or to reject the gospel.

HOW CAN I BE SAVED?

- Believe God loves you and wants your fellowship.
- Admit your rebellion and ask God's forgiveness.
- Believe Christ died for you.
- Invite Him into your life as Lord and Savior.

11

Would a Good God
Send People to Hell?

Does God punish sinners? Is there a real hell in eternity? These questions are often raised by unbelievers. I have had many people say to me, "I just don't believe that God would ever damn anyone forever and ever."

The reason for considering this objection is that it really has a hidden issue behind it. The person who doubts that God would punish sin is really saying, "Why do I need Jesus to 'save' me? Save me from what?" If there is no judgment, then the cross of Christ has no meaning in terms of God's redeeming grace. If we do not believe God punishes sin eternally, then what's all this urgency about salvation? We are left with a flimsy universalism—*universalism* being a technical term to describe the teaching that God will ultimately forgive everyone: All will be "saved." This teaching is a dangerous heresy which can destroy evangelism.

A Permissive God in a Permissive Age   The question of God's wrath is a very real issue in our day. Our generation has been reared on permissiveness. From child education to criminal law, we have been taught to believe that wrongdoing should not be punished. This lifestyle has affected our view of God. To multitudes of people, God is nothing more than a kind old man "up there"! Sort of a gentle grandfather who is very indulgent with His grandchildren. Therefore, many have come to believe that God will somehow, someway, let them off the hook come Judgment Day.

Hell Is Here, Not There   Others have removed the idea of an eternal hell by developing a theology which says hell is here and now. Sin's judgment comes in this life only. We reap what we sow temporarily but not eternally. In other words, we punish ourselves by making wrong choices in life.

How to Respond

Where do we begin with this problem? If indeed the problem is real and we meet a person who really sees no need to be "saved" because he thinks he'll squeeze in the back door of heaven somehow, then we must help him see the truth.

GOD IS LOVE

I begin by saying, "I agree with you that God is love. That's how the Bible defines God in 1 John 4:8. God is love. He is not, nor has He ever been, a big bully in the sky who delights in punishing sinners. He is not a cosmic voodoo witch doctor sticking pins in our doll! God is *love*."

God's Love Can Be His Judgment

However, we need to understand that just because God is love does not mean God is easy, permissive, or weak. Love is strong. It is the strength of the universe. God's love is persistent, and determined to reach man. God does not have two faces, one angry and the other smiling. It is a false idea and conception to think of an angry Judge on Mount Sinai and a loving Father on Mount Calvary. Beyond God's love is His wrath, but it is a characteristic of His holy love which demands that He punish sin. I believe God's wrath is the other side of God's love.

In Heaven, With an Unchanged Heart

Let me share another idea with you. Because God is a loving Father, He wants us to love and serve Him willingly and joyfully. In fact, heaven is an experience more than it is a place. It is the eternal experience of loving and serving God. That is the vocation and continuous occupation of the saved in heaven. Revelation 22:3, 4 reads, "And there shall no longer be any curse; and the throne of God and of the Lamb shall be in it, and His bond-servants shall serve Him: and they shall see His face, and His name shall be on their foreheads."

Just suppose God would let you into His presence without having your sins forgiven. Suppose you were to go to heaven without a changed heart, and all your guilt went with you. Do you think you would be happy in heaven? Never! You would hate it. Heaven would be hell to you! God's holiness would eat you alive! You'd be continually reminded of how you'd failed Him. Every time you looked at the Lord Jesus you would cringe from His look of love. Just like Isaiah in the temple when he saw the Lord God "high and lifted up," you'd cry out, "Woe is me! for I am undone; because I am a man of unclean lips." (Isaiah 6:5 KJV). God's holy love would be judgment for you.

Also, in heaven your only job is to serve God and to praise Him. If you have not had a disposition to serve and love God here on earth, what makes you think you'd enjoy serving Him there? He who doesn't enjoy praying, witnessing, worshiping, serving, and enjoying God here will hate heaven! My point is, you need a new-birth salvation experience to breathe the very air of heaven. Heaven would be hell for the lost sinner.

Love Is the Hell of It

Let me illustrate this another way. King David said, "If I make my bed in hell [Hebrew *Sheol*] . . . thou art there"

(Psalms 139:8 KJV). Now, in what sense is God in hell? I thought hell was a place of separation from God. Here is a remarkable truth; Hell is a separation from God's fellowship but not from God's presence. God is in hell; whatever or wherever hell is, He is there! Who is He? He is love! God's presence in hell is an everlasting reminder to those who rejected Jesus, that they blew off the love of God. And God will never let them forget it! To be eternally reminded that you missed out on the joy of a loving Father has got to be eternity's greatest torment! It would be heaven to those in hell if they could forget about God and John 3:16. But they cannot! Therefore, forget the idea that God is a two-faced God, sometimes loving and at other times vengeful. No, He is always loving—but that loving can be hell to those who rejected His love and are continually confronted with this magnificent love of God.

GOD IS HOLY

We need then to see that God is love, but His love gets its strength from His holiness. God is a righteous Judge of the Universe. He is not permissive with those who violate His laws. As a good Father, He lovingly seeks to correct us. If we refuse His discipline, He rebukes us. (*See* Revelation 3:19; Hebrews 12:6.)

Because God is holy, He must punish sin. Because He is love, He has no desire to punish sinners. (*See* Ezekiel 33:11 and 2 Peter 3:9.) God has met both demands of His character by sending His only Son Jesus to die for our sins on the cross. Jesus took our guilt and satisfied God's justice. He died for our sins. As 1 Peter 3:18 says, "For Christ also died for sins once for all, the just for the unjust, in order that He might bring us to God . . . ."

Double Jeopardy

Christ has paid the penalty for sins. The debt is paid. God loves us and can now rightfully forgive us and receive us. This is made possible through Jesus our Savior.

However, there is a condition. John 3:36 says, "He who believes in the Son has eternal life; but he who does not obey the Son shall not see life, but the wrath of God abides on him."

God's wrath still abides on those who do not trust in His Son. To die without Christ is to pay for your own sins. It is needless. It is double jeopardy. But it is true. Beyond the love of God in Christ is the wrath of God.

There Is an Experience Called Hell

Are you familiar with the story Jesus told of the rich man and the beggar Lazarus (Luke 16:19—31)? This story from the lips of Jesus should settle the issue once and for all. He told this story to warn us of the folly of rejecting salvation. After a lost sinner dies there comes judgment (Hebrews, 9:27). There is a "great gulf fixed" (*see* Luke 16:26). This destiny is permanent. Make no mistake about it: There is an experience Jesus calls *hell*.

Is There Literally Fire in Hell?

Frequently I am asked, "Surely, you don't believe there is literally fire in hell?"

Let me answer that question this way: First, God has a fire that does not consume. Moses saw God in a flaming bush, and the bush burned but was not consumed. God does have an everlasting fire.

Secondly, if fire is only a symbol of the horror of hell, then we must realize that a symbol is only a shadow of the reality it symbolizes. The reality is always greater than the symbol. If fire is only a symbol, then think how much greater the real horror of hell must be! It must be a greater torment than real fire! I don't know what hell is exactly, I just know that Jesus described it so well I don't want to go there—ever! I want Him to be my Savior and take me home with Him when I die.

ONLY ONE SIN DAMNS US

What sins do we commit that are so terrible as to send us to hell? None! This needs to be understood. God doesn't send people to hell for sins. It is not a penitentiary of the damned. God doesn't send us to hell. We choose our destiny, God doesn't. There is only one requirement for hell—unbelief. Only one sin damns us—unbelief. John 3:18, 19 says it well: "There is no eternal doom awaiting those who trust him to save them. But those who don't trust him have already been tried and condemned for not believing in the only Son of God. Their sentence is based on this fact: that the Light from heaven came into the world, but they loved the darkness more than the Light, for their deeds were evil" (LB).

Jesus has already taken our hell. To reject Him is to sentence yourself to an eternity without God's forgiveness.

12

What About Those Who Have Never Heard of Christ?

This question is often asked in various forms: What about the heathen? Are Muslims, Buddhists, and Hindus doomed to hell because they don't believe in Jesus Christ?

An international student from Iran recently said to me, "We Muslims worship the same God you do, only we call Him by a different name."

Was my Muslim friend correct, or is Jesus Christ the *only* way to God? Christ Himself made such an exclusive claim when He declared, *"I am the way, and the truth, and the life; no one comes to the Father, but through Me"* (John 14:6). How can I explain this statement to the Muslim or Hindu? This is a difficult question and it needs an in-depth answer.

Some Basic Spiritual Laws

- *God Is Love*—1 John 4:8: ". . . for God is love."

  The Bible clearly states that God is a loving Father who desires all men to have fellowship with Him. He wills that all men be saved. In 2 Peter 3:9 we are told that God is ". . . not willing that any should perish . . ." (KJV). And 1 Timothy 2:4 declares that God ". . . desires all men to be saved."

- *God Is Just*—Job 34:12: "Surely, God will not act wickedly, And the Almighty will not pervert justice."

  We must not accuse God of being unfair. The Scriptures reveal God as the just Judge of the unwise. He will always deal fairly with each man.

- *Everyone Who Desires Salvation Shall Find It*

  Acts 8:26 and following verses describe an African eunuch who was reading Isaiah 53 but could not understand its meaning. He was a sincere "pagan" seeking to know the truth. God brought Phillip the evangelist to him to point out the meaning of the Scriptures. Here is a great biblical principle: No one has ever remained lost and without Christ who really wanted to be found. God will see to it that every seeker after truth finds the truth. God will bring a Phillip into every seeker's life.

HOW IGNORANT IS THE HEATHEN?

As we consider those who have never heard of Christ, we must not assume they have not heard of God. Are some men "ignorant" of the truth of God? Romans 1:19 says no, they are not! This passage confirms that all men have some knowledge of God, because God has made Himself known to them. Paul says God reveals Himself in at least two ways.

Nature Reveals God

God is seen through nature. We call this natural revelation. Romans 1:20 reads, "For since the creation of the world His invisible attributes, His eternal power and divine nature, have been clearly seen, being understood through what has been made, so that they are without excuse."

What a statement! Paul says the "heathen" is without

excuse. Why? Because the universe testifies to its Creator, so men know about His existence.

Nature Argues for a First Cause   "His eternal power" is seen in nature. Every man has asked, "Who or what started the universe? How did it all begin?" The universe demands an explanation for its origin. Our basic response to this question is to believe there exists an "eternal power" which created it all.

Nature Argues for a Designer   Paul says again that the universe reveals God's "divine nature." What he means is that when we observe the universe we see design and purpose. The natural world has natural laws. This structure and design indicates to each of us that whoever or whatever power created us, is a thinking, planning divine architect. If this eternal power can think and design, then it is a personal power. This is why primitive man worships a *god* not an *it*. We even speak of "Mother Nature," because we feel that nature is personal.

The Psalmist said, "The heavens are telling the glory of God and the firmament is declaring the work of his hands" (*see* Psalms 19:1).

The Law Within Reveals God

Notice Paul says that our knowledge of God is not only from without (nature) but also from "within." Romans 1:19 says it is "evident *within them*." Paul explains this "inward" knowledge in chapter 2 of Romans when he says, ". . . they show the work of the Law written in their hearts, their conscience bearing witness . . ." (verse 15).

Now where did conscience come from? The Bible sees it as the evidence of "natural law" inside every human heart. *Natural Law* is the term C. S. Lewis uses to describe conscience in man. Lewis has written an excellent chapter on this subject in *The Case for Christianity*. Because we are created in the image of God, possessing a spirit which is unique to humankind, there is in all of us an inward moral code. This moral code is a call upward for each of us. It is evidence of God's existence which we know instinctively.

This Law Within Manifests Itself Two Ways:

• *The Divine* Oughtness *Spurs Conscience*

Each man knows he *ought* to do right. When he doesn't do right, he feels guilt. His conscience accuses him. Even if he breaks a simple tribal rule, he is accused and feels real guilt.

• *The* Oughtness *Is a Call to Love*

All human laws and tribal rules are in response to the natural law within. It is the law of love. God created us with an *oughtness* to love. When we do not love, we feel guilt. This is shown to be true in that nowhere in human society is selfishness seen to be a virtue. All men feel they ought to be unselfish.

Now, where did this inward oughtness to love originate? It is a gift from God, who *is* love. It is an inward "light" that lights every human heart so men will seek Him.

The "Ignorant" Savage

The poor pagan in the jungle doesn't sound so ignorant any longer, does he? You read Romans 1:19 and see if you don't agree with the apostle Paul that they knew God! So you see, God has not left anyone in spiritual darkness, damned and doomed. God has revealed Himself through nature and conscience as an eternal, personal, moral God. Therefore, we are "without excuse."

SOME PRINCIPLES TO WORK BY

Having established that God is just and has not left men in darkness, there are some principles for us to consider regarding people who have not heard of Jesus Christ. Let's consider the following:

All Men Have Some "Light" From God   Our previous discussion of Romans chapter 1, has confirmed the fact that all men have some "light" from God.

Light Received Brings the Promise of More Light   In Romans 4:20–22 we read of Abraham's journey with God. Abraham is an illustration of a man who responded in faith to what little he knew about God. He didn't even know God's name, yet he followed God's will. God in response to Abraham's obedience revealed more of Himself to Abraham. God will do the same for anyone who desires to know Him. If you respond in faith to what you know intuitively, God will lead you to a full knowledge of Himself in Jesus Christ.

However, faith is the key to heaven's door. Hebrews 11:6 says that "he who comes to God must *believe* that he is . . ." (italics added). God honors faith. It is to be our only approach.

Light Rejected Brings Darkness and Judgment   Most men and nations have not responded in faith as Abraham did. We have turned the revealed truth of God into a lie (Romans 1:25). Therefore, the wrath of God is upon those who suppress the truth.

John 3:19 states this fact: "And this is the judgment, that the light is come into the world, and men loved the darkness rather than the light; for their deeds were evil." This statement affirms that multitudes of people are under the judgment of God. They love darkness and don't want to receive the "light." But, God has offered it.

Perverted Truth

What about the great religions of the world? Do the Muslim and the Buddhist worship God in truth? No, they do not. Romans 1:12–25 tells us that religion is a perversion of truth. Rather than worship God in faith and obedience, mankind has substituted religion. Religion is futile speculation of which Paul speaks in Romans 1:21. He calls it futile, or empty, reasoning.

Why is religion not acceptable? Because religion is based on human effort and works. Every religion known to man declares that the way to please God is through works, ritual, and sacrifice. The Hindu calls it good karma. This is not God's way. We are to come to God in simple faith as Abraham did. God declared Abraham righteous because he believed, not because he was good.

Religion is a poor substitute for a relationship with the living God. Nothing in all this world has suppressed the truth about God as has religion! *Professing himself to be wise, religious man has proved himself to be a fool. (See* Romans 1:22.)

Now, not only does light suppressed bring judgment, but God's judgment is different for different individuals.

God's Judgment Is Based Upon the Light Received There are degrees of punishment in God's economy. Jesus taught this principle in Luke 12:47, 48: *"And that slave who knew his master's will and did not get ready or act in accord with his will, shall receive many lashes, but the one who did not know it, and committed deeds worthy of a flogging, will receive but few. And from everyone who has been given much shall much be required; and to whom they entrusted much, of him they will ask all the more"* (italics added).

These words teach us that God is just. His judgments are fair. Thus, the man who knows about God only through nature and conscience will not be judged as severely as the person who has heard of Christ's love and has rejected the gospel. To him much has been given, of him shall much be required. Which leads me to say that often when someone asks me, "What about the heathen?" I am inclined to say, "What about you? What have *you* done with Jesus Christ?

Have you accepted Him as your Savior?" If you are so concerned about those people who haven't heard about Christ,
what are you doing to tell them about Him? It seems that
this objection is often raised not out of genuine concern for
others but as a smoke screen to evade one's own responsibility to let Jesus become Lord.

Jesus Christ Is God's Second Chance for Sinners　In
John 14:6 Jesus tells us He is the way to the Father. Notice,
He is *the* way, not *a* way.

There is no evidence that anyone has ever been saved
apart from the shed blood of Jesus Christ. How then was
Abraham saved if he never heard of Christ? He was saved
by faith in the limited "light" that he had. God looked down
through the years of history and deposited the blood of His
Son Jesus to Abraham's account. All the Old Testament
"saints" were saved by faith, and the God who transcends
time accounted the cross to their cause. Everyone who has
ever found God to be a merciful Father has walked into
God's presence through the blood of Jesus Christ. (*See* Hebrews 9:22.)

Hearing the Gospel Increases Responsibility　John 3:19
tells us we are judged by the light we have. If you have
heard the gospel of Jesus Christ and have not received
Him, you will be judged by Him. How great a damnation
for those who have despised the blood of God's Son. God's
greater wrath is upon those who will fully reject His Son.
(*See* Hebrews 10:28, 29.)

TELL THE WORLD IN ONE GENERATION

If we are really concerned about the heathen, we need to
be reminded that God had made it possible for all men in
any one generation to know of His love and forgiveness. If
Christians would faithfully share the good news with
others, it is mathematically possible to share Christ with
every human being in a few short years. We are the light of
the world, and God wills it that all men know His Son.

13

What Is Predestination?

A semester never passes but that some student says to me, "What difference does it make whether I accept Christ or not? Everything is predestined anyway. If I'm meant to go to heaven, I will—and if I'm not, then I can't change anything." Behind this statement is a great deal of confusion over the meaning of some big theological words such as *predestination, election,* and *foreknowledge.* Just what is predestination? Does it mean that God has already made out the list of who's to be saved and who isn't?

In answering this question it is only necessary for us to understand one passage of Scripture—Romans 8:28–31. It is this passage that has caused so much discussion on this subject. Romans 8:29 is the fly in the ointment. It reads, "For whom He foreknew, He also predestined to become conformed to the image of His Son, that He might be the first-born among many brethren . . . ."

WHAT PREDESTINATION IS NOT

This passage does not mean that God has planned in advance who will go to heaven and who will go to hell. At the time America was going through her birth as a nation the argument about predestination was very heated. A group called *hypercalvinists* held that God had so willed salvation for His "elect" that their salvation was inevitable. This group was very antievangelistic. Billy Graham definitely does not fit their mold! Why go to all the trouble to witness if the lost are "bound" to be saved regardless of the Church's efforts? This extreme position destroys all initiative for outreach to people who do not know Christ. Whatever *predestination* means, it does not mean fatalism. "Allah has willed it" may be fine for the Muslim, but it is not for the Christian.

WHAT IS MEANT BY "PREDESTINATION"?

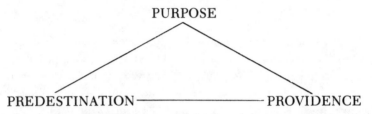

PURPOSE

PREDESTINATION ———————————— PROVIDENCE

In explaining Romans 8:28–31, I find it helps to illustrate it as a triangle. Notice that the apex of the triangle is the *purpose* of God. Everything God does comes forth from the apex of His divine purpose for us. Verse 28 says God causes everything to work out for the good of those who are *called according to His purpose.* In explaining predestination, notice two things:

These Words Are Written to Christians   We, the saved, are "those who love God" and are "called." Therefore everything Paul says about predestination applies only to those who are already saved. The Bible nowhere says the lost person is predestined to go to hell or heaven. The Greek word for *predestination* literally means to "mark off" or to determine beforehand.

These Words Tell Us God's Purpose For the Christian Verse 29 tells us God's purpose for us is that we may be conformed to the image of His Son. In other words, once we are saved, God has only one purpose for us: to make us like His Son Jesus. God is so determined to fulfill His purpose that He has "marked us off," determined beforehand to accomplish His purpose. Nothing can keep God from making us like Jesus—"If God be for us, who can be against us?" (Romans 8:31 KJV).

You'll never understand predestination and election apart from the purpose of God. God's purpose is that all men be saved. He desires everyone to know and to be like His Son (1 Timothy 2:4). This is His one purpose for the human family.

PREDESTINATION ASSURES THE PURPOSE OF GOD

Because God wants you to be saved, Paul says, "He determined beforehand to call you" (*see* Romans 8:30). After He called you (and He does call every man) He then justified you. This means that as you respond in repentance and faith to His call, you are forgiven, based upon the work of Jesus on the cross. He then is so determined to fulfill His purpose that He has already, in His own mind, seen you as "glorified" (already in heaven, made like Jesus)!

How Does Predestination Work?

By Getting Us Saved in the First Place Again look at verse 30. God's purpose is that we be conformed to the image of His Son. How does God fulfill that purpose? He determines before I am born to call me. This He does. His predeterminate will to call me assured that He would call me. Ephesians 1:4 says: ". . . just as He chose us in Him before the foundation of the world, that we should be holy and blameless before Him."

Balancing Predestination and Free Will How do you leave room for man's free will to accept or reject God's call? We must admit this is a difficult thing to understand. Just read Romans chapters 9 through 11 and see if Paul understood it. He didn't! He was left with a paradox: "Jacob have I [God] loved, but Esau have I hated" (Romans 9:13 KJV).

However, there is a key to working out this puzzle. Read again Ephesians 1:4: ". . . Just as He chose us *in Him* . . . ." That phrase *in Him* is the qualifying phrase. God chooses people only when they are "in Him." He calls everyone; He chooses and elects only those who choose to *accept* His call.

A Predestined Airplane   A simple illustration may help. At the airport sits a plane which will leave for New York City. It is preplanned that this particular plane will fly there. It is scheduled to do so. The moment I get on that plane, I too am determined to go to New York. When I am on the plane, then everything that was preplanned for the plane becomes true for me as well. I am predestined, as the plane was, to go to New York.

Now, predestination and election apply only to those who accept God's call to receive Christ. The moment you accept Christ, you are "in Him." You can accept or reject Jesus—you are free to choose. God calls you, but it is not irresistible grace—you *can* resist; you *can* stay off the plane. If you do not get on the plane, then the predestination plans for the plane will not affect you. Even so with God's predestination: It applies only to those who accept it.

Predestination Assures Me of Being Saved in the Last Place   Jesus said, "No one can come to Me unless the Father who sent Me draws him; and I will raise him up *on the last day*" (John 6:44, italics added). Jesus is saying that the moment you respond to God's call, God is predetermined to make you like Jesus and ultimately assure salvation "on the last day."

Where Does God's Foreknowledge Come In?

The most difficult question to answer is about God's foreknowledge. If God knew a person would not accept Jesus, then did the person have a real option to accept or not? Yes, he did. Because what God *knows* and what He *wills* are not the same thing. God wills everyone to be saved, therefore He calls everyone. He calls some even though He knows they will not accept. It grieves Him, but He does not and did not choose for them to reject. Secondly, those whom He foreknows will accept Christ; these He determines to help even before they are born. I know this is a mind bender but we humans, in our limited knowledge, must wrestle with the profundity of God's ways with us.

GOD'S PROVIDENCE SERVES HIS PURPOSE

Let's review the triangle: God's purpose is the apex. Everything God does with man is aimed at fulfilling His purpose. For those who God knows will accept His purpose, He goes to work, determined beforehand to carry it out. Then providence takes over.

What Is Divine Providence?

The root of the word *providence* is *provide*. God provides for the Christian adequate means to carry out His purpose. Providence is God looking into the future knowing what is going to happen to us, then making plans to bring it to pass with the idea that He will use our happenings to fulfill His purpose. That's the point of Romans 8:28. He is working (providing) all things to our good.

Providence and Predestination

The difference between predestination and providence is the difference between certainty and necessity. Certainty is predestination. There are certain things God wills beforehand to happen to us. There are other things that happen that God does not directly will to happen but which He permits to happen. Providence is God's watchcare, using my circumstances to my good.

CONCLUSION

This subject is difficult but worthy of our understanding because it tells us of our Heavenly Father's love and good wishes toward us. He is constantly working every thing to our good. If He is for us, who can be against us? This truth is profound for the lost man. It says, "You do not have to be lost. God is for you, working to call you to Himself. You do not have to stay the way you are." The Christian witness must be able to explain this truth to the unbeliever so that he can see the goodness of God. He too must enter into God's purpose for His life, so God can go to work in him and through him.

14

Jesus and the Gurus

One has only to go to any airport in one of America's major cities or walk across the campus of one of our large universities to encounter a guru or one of his followers. Hare Krishna is on Main Street U.S.A., and Buddha is offering flowers in the suburbs. Transcendental Meditation is passed off as a science and taught in the classroom for a fee. America, the Christian nation, has its other gurus besides Jesus. Indeed, some new sects teach that Jesus went to Tibet for His enlightenment at the feet of some ancient guru! East and West have met head on. Therefore, the Christian witness should heed the challenge of Peter, "always being ready to make a defense to every one who asks you to give an account for the hope that is in you . . ." (1 Peter 3:15). One can not witness to the international student on campus or to any person who has a Hindu or Buddhist background without some fundamental knowledge of what these Eastern religions believe. Our purpose in this chapter is threefold: First, to give a brief historical background of the major Eastern religions; secondly, to state the major teaching of these religions with a biblical refutation; then finally to present a method for sharing Christ with those whose religion is Eastern in origin.

WHO ARE THE GURUS?

Names like Gautama, Mahauira, Nanak, Dyananda Saras-
vati, Confucius, Amida Buddha, Gandhi, "The Bab," and
Reverend Moon, mean little or nothing to most Christians.
However, these names are legend to millions of devout
followers. They are the divine gurus, the enlightened ones.
The great majority of the world's population follows the
teachings of these "seers." Because the guru has come to
America, it is imperative that the evangelical Christian understand the thought patterns of these leaders.

Hinduism: The Mother of the East

India, the world's most populated country, is 50 percent
Hindu! *Hindu* is a Persian word meaning Indian. Thus
Hinduism is simply a term describing the religious beliefs
of the Indian people. Oldest of the world's religions, Hinduism is like the mighty Amazon River. It has many
tributaries branching off it. Buddhism, Jainism, Sikhism,
and many others are all Hindu heresies or reform move-
ments. If we can understand the basic teaching of this
mother of Eastern religions, we can then deal with the
character traits of her offspring.

Hinduism and Evolving Thought

All religion is fundamentally man's philosophy about
God and the universe. Religion is men's musing about life
and its purpose. Hinduism is essentially the collected
thoughts of seekers after God. Hindu scholar R. C. Zachner
in his book *Hinduism* (London, Oxford University Press,
1962) divides Hinduism into four distinct periods of evolv-
ing thought about God:

The Period of the Rig-Veda   These ancient books of hymns are very polytheistic and view the world as filled with many gods.

The Period of Pantheism   This period of Hindu philosophy viewed God as equal to nature, but God as one, the supreme god among many others.

The Period of Vishnu and Siva   This thought views Vishnu as the good god and Siva as a more evil deity. Both are elevated to supreme reality during this period in Hindu religious philosophy.

The Modern Era   Zachner says we are now in a modern era of continued reform with much emphasis upon the worth and spiritual essence of the individual.

Hindu Scripture—Guru Guessings

None of the ancient Eastern religions claims that its scriptures are the divine word of God as does the Judaeo-Christian faith. Because the Hindu concept of God is impersonal, God does speak to men in oracles. Hindu scripture is man's thoughts about God, it is more philosophy than scripture. I call it guru guessings about goodness and the gods.

The Rig-Veda   Hindu's oldest literature. It is ancient hymns to the nature gods. The Rig-Veda was written from oral tradition in the eighth century B.C.

The Vedas   The vedas are a large body of writings which includes the Samhitas, Brahmanas, and Upanishads:

- The Samhitas—a collection of sacred hymns and wisdom.
- The Brahmanas—priestly writings dealing primarily with priestly functions and the sacrificial ceremony used by Hindu priests of the eighth century B.C.

- The Bhagavad-Gita—the most popular of all Hindu literature. This "Song of the Lord" contains a higher concept of God as deity than earlier writings. It speaks of God's love for humanity and man's response to God.

There is a very obvious progression in religious thought in later literature as opposed to the primitive nature gods of the Rig-Veda. The more current literature moves toward monotheism as a concept of God as love. I recommend that the Christian who desires to witness to the Eastern mind familiarize himself with this literature. The Christian must note the date of writing and its authorship to get some idea of the background of the literature. A good source book for beginning to read Hindu thought is *Hinduism* by Louis Renou.

WHAT DOES THE GURU BELIEVE?

Rather than a detailed account of the teachings of Hinduism it is probably better to have an understanding of some general teachings of all Eastern religion. Generally speaking, the Hindu, Buddhist, and all their cousins will share these common doctrinal kinships. Later in this chapter we will look at Buddhism separately with its unique American versions.

Hare Krishna

Surely you've seen these young people on the streets with their yellow robes, shaven heads, and strange chanting music. They are worshiping Krishna, a Hindu god. This Krishna cult is an offshoot of mainstream Hinduism. The doctrines we shall look at all apply to this group and most others. What do they believe?

EASTERN THOUGHT VS. BIBLICAL REVELATION

Eastern Thought

Biblical Revelation

PANTHEISM

A TRANSCENDENT CREATOR

Hindu thought says that all reality is Brahman. Brahman is the impersonal god who is all things. Everything is god and god is everything. Therefore, all created reality is sacred to the Hindu. They call it "reverence for life." The natural conclusion from this is that man is divine—a chip off the ol' block!

God was before creation; He is creation but is independent of it, though He sustains it. Genesis 1 and 2 affirm the difference between who God is and what He created.

ATMAN: IMMORTALITY OF THE SOUL

THE GIFT OF ETERNAL LIFE

Man is made of the divine essence which is Brahman. This essence in man is called *atman*. Atman is the soul in man. It is trapped in the cage of our body. It is immortal and can never die. Atman needs to be released to become one with Brahman.

The Bible says that only God is eternal. The soul of man is not eternal and is not of the same essence as God. The Bible says that the soul that sins shall die, but the gift of God is eternal life by means of resurrection.

MAYA: ILLUSION

BIBLICAL REALISM

Basic to all Eastern thought is the concept of *maya*. *Maya* means illusion. Everything the five senses

The Bible asserts the realness of creation. God told Adam to "subdue" the earth. This is why science has

Eastern Thought

reveal to us as material reality is an illusion. There is no "realness" to things. Only Brahman is real, and all things are Brahman. Sin to the Hindu is nothing but ignorance of maya. Sin is the illusion that this life is real. Salvation is gaining the truth that all is maya and escaping this illusion into the real world of the spirit. For example, I am sitting in a chair, but the chair is not a chair. The chair is an illusion. The chair is no different from me—we are both Brahman. All things are spiritual, and truth comes when I see my "oneness" with all things.

KARMA

The law of *karma* is a belief common to many Eastern religions. Karma decrees that every act has its appropriate result. Good acts create good karma, bad acts create bad karma. The law of karma is primary of Hindu and Buddhist teaching, especially when karma is linked with reincarnation,

Biblical Revelation

flourished under Judaeo-Christian thought; we believe that God created a real world for us to use and enjoy. India will never excel in science because you don't study what is an illusion. Secondly, the Bible doesn't agree with the concept of the oneness of created things. God created each species "after its kind," unique and different. Thirdly, sin is more than ignorance of illusion—it is a rebellion against a loving Father.

GRACE

The Bible agrees that sin brings its own reward (Galatians 6:7, 8) and that good deeds make for a happier life. However, Christian faith denies that human works are the means to salvation (Titus 3:5). Rather, that faith in a personal Savior can change the results of "bad karma." Grace

Eastern Thought

as in Hinduism. To the Eastern mind, good karma (works) is the door of escape from the cycle of reincarnation. Bad karma dooms us to rebirth in a lower form of life! Salvation is entirely based on human deeds— good karma. Brahman (god) to the Hindu is primarily a faceless bookkeeper, although he may be incarnate himself at times (as Vishnu).

REINCARNATION

Transmigration of the soul is a basic concept of Eastern religion. The atman, or soul, is immortal. It is released from the human body at death. (Some say reincarnation takes place forty-nine days after death. See the Buddhist work *The Tibetan Book of the Dead*.) The goal of life is to escape reincarnation and achieve absorption of the soul into oneness with Brahman. Achieving this absorption seldom happens, and reincarnation is the destiny of man. The only es-

Biblical Revelation

and forgiveness are possible. Also, salvation is not escape from reincarnation but a personal fellowship with the Living God here and now, and the hope of resurrection in the future. The fundamental difference from Hinduism is that Christianity is based upon what a personal God did for us, and Eastern thought is based upon what man does for God. (*See* Romans 3:19–22.)

RESURRECTION

The Bible rejects the transmigration of the soul and any idea of reincarnation:

(1) Christianity asserts the uniqueness of each person. You are not a body with a soul, you are an individual, a person. A person is a totality of being—spirit, soul, and body (1 Thessalonians 5:23).

(2) You will not pass this way again. "It is appointed for men to die once" (Hebrews 9:27).

(3) You will not lose your

Eastern Thought

cape from reincarnation into Nirvana is good karma (only after many reincarnations).

Biblical Revelation

identity after death. King David, facing the death of his little child, is sorrowful but not without hope. He says, "But now that he has died, why should I fast? . . . I shall go to him, but he will not return to me" (*see* 2 Samuel 12:23).

(4) Your destiny is fixed at death: heaven or hell. Jesus said to the thief on the cross, "Today you shall be with Me in Paradise" (Luke 23:43). Paul said, "To be absent from the body is to be present with the Lord" (*see* 2 Corinthians 5:8).

(5) Your salvation is not dependent upon what you do (karma) but upon what God does (grace).

(6) Your ultimate destiny with God is not static, but dynamic. In Christianity, we believe that heaven is not absorption but service. Revelation 22:3 says, ". . . his servants shall serve Him" (KJV). Eternity is a growing experience for the Christian; not a mindless, personless oneness with God.

Eastern Thought	*Biblical Revelation*
VIEW OF HISTORY: CIRCULAR	**VIEW OF HISTORY: REDEMPTIVE**
Man, like the planet earth, is going nowhere, only in circles. Life is an endless struggle. Reincarnation is the expression of this struggle. History has no purpose or meaning. It is only a revolving stage upon which this drama of life is played.	The Bible teaches that God is working in the affairs of men and governments, working out His ultimate goal—the Kingdom of God. We Christians are taught to pray "Thy kingdom come . . . ." Life does have meaning and there are no accidents in history. God is in charge. Hebrews 1:3 says of Christ that He "upholds all things by the word of His power."
NIRVANA	**SALVATION AND HEAVEN**
Hindu thought cherishes the idea of escape from life into *nirvana,* or absorption of the atman with Brahman. It is release from reincarnation. This "heaven" to the Hindu is based on the caste system of India. The better your karma, the higher your next reincarnation. You move higher up in caste each time until you reach the priestly level. The priest is just a step away from nirvana. He is a holy man, a guru. This mystic oneness, attained through yoga medi-	(1) The Christian faith affirms that life here and now can and should have meaning. We are to be responsible citizens seeking with God's help to face life, not to escape it. (2) Our ultimate destiny is to experience fellowship with our Heavenly Father—not absorption into the Godhead, losing identity. (3) Heaven is not our ultimate experience. The Kingdom of God, with a new heaven and a new earth

Eastern Thought

tation and discipline, is fully attained at death into nirvana. Buddhist thought rejects the idea of immortality and could even be said to be atheistic. Yet Buddhists believe that Gautama, the Buddha, became an incarnation of the god Vishnu. Nirvana is achieved in one of three ways:

(1) Through works (karma yoga) like studying the vedas and showing kindness to others.

(2) Through knowledge (jnana yoga) gained by deep meditation.

(3) Through devotion (bhakti yoga), worshiping God.

THE AVATARS

Many Eastern religions believe that the god or gods manifest themselves in human or animal forms called *avatars*. These avatars are divine visitors or mediators to man who come to help in time of need.

Biblical Revelation

where Christ shall rule is our goal.

(4) Jesus has gone to prepare a special place for us, showing our special destiny (2 John 14:1).

ONE MEDIATOR BETWEEN GOD AND MAN

"For there is one God, and one mediator also between God and men, the man Christ Jesus" (1 Timothy 2:5). We as Christians need to share with others that God has once and for all time come to our aid, not in an avatar, but in a Son. Jesus is not an avatar, He is the Son of God, "only begotten." There is no need of another.

Eastern Thought

Biblical Revelation

GURUS

Because of the great emphasis on yoga and the need for "enlightenment" in Eastern thought, there is a reverence for the "holy man" in all Eastern religion. The guru has been through many reincarnations to reach the level where he is now. This is why he is revered. His disciplined life is a challenge and an example to the people. Historically many teachers (gurus) have reinterpreted Hindu thought and led in reforms. Buddhism began as a reform by Gautama in the fifth century B.C. against the caste system. Nanak in the sixteenth century founded Sikhism, which is an attempt to harmonize Hinduism and Islam. The guru is continually changing the face of Eastern deity.

JESUS THE CHRIST

(1) Christianity is unique in that it offers the world an eternal, changeless Christ. Jesus is more than guru or teacher. He is the timeless Christ, the cornerstone of truth. Christianity does not follow the latest "thinker" or holy man. Our faith is built on nothing less than Jesus' blood and righteousness.

(2) It is important to show those in Eastern religion the uniqueness of Christ, His historical sacrificial death, and primarily the significance of His Resurrection. The empty tomb is a mind bender to the Hindu-Buddhist mind. (*See* 1 Corinthians 15:3, 4.)

(3) Christianity is built upon *who* Jesus is, not just upon what He taught. He offers *Himself* to the believer, not just an ethic or code. The guru comes and dies; he offers only words and ideas. Not so with Jesus the Christ.

Witnessing to the Eastern Mind

We have looked at the beliefs which are common to most Eastern religions. It is not our purpose to deal with each sect individually. This would require an entire book (and many such have been written). If as a Christian witness you encounter an individual involved in some Americanized version of Buddhism, like Nichiren Shoshu, you'll find that further study may be necessary. (Nichiren was a thirteenth-century Japanese Buddhist who taught that allegiance to guru Amida Buddha was the one true religion. The lay organization of Nichiren Shoshu is called Soka Gakkai. There are 30,000 of this group in the United States.) Each of these versions has its own beliefs and history, but even the general background given here will help you to assist your witness to the guru groups.

- Inform yourself on the background of the person you are sharing with.
- Seek to understand his perspective. For example, the Hindu tends to be very eclectic. He wants to include Jesus in the pantheon of his gods. You must show him your perspective of the uniqueness of Jesus.
- What is his position religiously? Is he an orthodox Hindu, Buddhist, et cetera? Is he only casually or culturally religious?
- Seek to find the points of agreement, such as the problem of suffering. This is the focal point of all Eastern thought: Why do we suffer? How can we escape it? This is where Buddha began, and this is where the Christian and Eastern can meet for discussion. (*See* chapter 9, "Why Does God Allow Evil and Suffering?")
- Realize that the great obstacle is the concept of world soul and reincarnation. The Resurrection of Christ is the great hang-up to the Buddhist (who does not be-

lieve in immortality). Yet the Resurrection is our hope, and we must share the personhood and work of Christ with the compassion and conviction.

- Share the idea that sin is internal (the sin nature) rather than deeds or outward actions. Salvation means a changed heart, not just outward acts.
- Above all, be a tender, patient loving friend to the international. Show the love of Christ; then you will speak volumes as a Christian.

RECOMMENDED SUPPLEMENTAL READING

Buddhism and Christianity by Winston L. King (Philadelphia: Westminster Press, 1962)

Contemporary Religions in Japan, September 1965, article by James Allen Dator: "The Soka Gakkai: A Socio Political Interpretation"

Hinduism (London: Oxford University Press, 1962)

Introducing Buddhism by Kenneth Scott Latourette (New York: Friendship Press, 1956)

Leading Religions of the World by Max Stilson (Grand Rapids: Zondervan Publishing House, 1964)

The Life of Buddha as Legend and History by Edward J. Thomas (New York: Alfred A. Knopf, 1933)

The World's Religions by Charles S. Braden (New York: Abingdon Press, 1954)

Further information can also be had by writing: The American Buddhist Association, 1151 West Leland Avenue, Chicago, Illinois, and Followers of Buddha, 60 Las Encinas Lane, Santa Barbara, California.

15

Jesus and the Gay Community

"Kiss a Fairy for Jesus" was on a church sign recently in Florida, celebrating Gay Liberation Week in the church. In Hollywood, California, hundreds of gay couples worship weekly in the world's largest homosexual church, the Metropolitan Community Church, relates its pastor, Troy D. Perry, in his autobiography *The Lord Is My Shepherd and He Knows I'm Gay* (Nash Publications, Los Angeles, 1972). Marriages between gays are performed regularly. Gay Power parades in our major cities tell us the homosexuals are here in unashamed splendor.

Time magazine (September 20, 1976) carried an article by a Father McNeill in which he advocated that the Roman Catholic Church should welcome the gays as nonsinners; he even quoted Scripture to support his theology. One admirer of Father MacNeill's progay theology said in a letter to the editor (*Time,* October 1, 1976) "Homosexual love is a celebration of the love of God. Gay is more than good; it is essential, necessary, and holy."

Archie Bunker and the Gays

What are we to think of all this? There seem to be three extreme positions regarding homosexual love. The oldest and most traditional is characterized by Archie Bunker of TV fame. Many, even within the Church, would applaud

134

Archie as he calls the homosexual every barroom name in his limited vocabulary—fag, fairy, pervert. It has been the attitude of too many church members just to relegate the gay to the category of rapist, Nazi, and antichrist.

The Ostrich Posture

Another group, largely within the Church, has sought just to ignore the problem. This was easy to do as long as the homosexual just took a closet profile. However, it's too late for that now—the masks are off, the gays are out in the open. The head-in-the-sand ostrich posture won't do any longer. People want to know, What does the Church think? Too often we haven't thought about it at all. That's the purpose of this chapter. Jesus and His family have a message for the gay community. I'm afraid the message isn't "kiss a fairy for Jesus," which seems to be the third attitude prescribed by some like Father McNeill. This is no solution, it is only surrender. It is my experience that the gays do not need our praise so much as they need our prayers.

Where to Begin

There is very little material in print by evangelicals which considers the gay problem from a truly biblical view. To my knowledge there is nothing in print which prepares the Christian witness to share the love of Christ with the homosexual. Because the gay mind is a unique entity, our witness to him must be unique and effective. He can be helped, not by patting him (or her) on the back and saying "Jesus loves you as you are," but rather by presenting the claims of Christ in love and understanding.

The Laboratory of Life

A word of personal testimony may help to qualify me as adequate to speak on this subject. Every pastor has felt his inadequacy when trying to help a gay person. When I came as pastor to a church in Hollywood, California, several years ago, I was totally unprepared for the Sunset Strip street life I was to encounter. I had been pastor there just a few weeks when I discovered there were at least six homosexuals singing in the choir. As these men and women came to me for counseling I realized my ignorance of this problem. However, after seven years of endless hours of ministry, I feel I have learned some principles worthy of sharing with others.

"God Can't Help Me"

One night I was talking to a young man on Sunset Boulevard, near Beverly Hills. He was in his twenties, neatly dressed and courteous to me as I talked to him about his relationship to God. He said, "I'm sorry, preacher, but God can't help me. My problem is beyond help. I tried Jesus and it didn't work." At that moment I realized he was homosexual. He, like others, had tried to change but had failed. He thought God was unable to help. He had committed himself to stay as he was.

This is the attitude of most gays. They either do not wish to be heterosexual, or they have no hope of being other than they are. Tragically, the "professional" world of psychology and medicine has not helped much. The consensus of opinion among psychiatrists is "leave them alone." In the midst of his failure to transform the gay into a "straight," the psychiatrist has surrendered and labeled the homosexual as nondeviant. However, to call something normal does not make it so, any more than changing the label on a bottle of poison makes it any less lethal.

The homosexual may have received the seal of approval from many people, but I think he is still bent on a path of self-destruction. Studies on suicide have in fact revealed the high frequency of suicide among homosexuals. In more than 50 percent of cases of suicide studied, homosexual tendencies were uncovered, says William A. O'Connor in "Some Notes on Suicide," *British Journal of Medical Psychology.* In any event, there are few "happy homos" in our world. They may call themselves *gay,* but that is the biggest misnomer in the English language. Statistics do not back it up. The gay life is a self-destructive process.

Hope for Those Who Want It

My purpose is to show the homosexual that there is a better life for him. He must not stay the way he is because it is a dead-end street. Secondly, God is able to deliver him from his bondage. Let me say right now to any gay person who may be reading these pages, that you must make up your mind and decide if you want God's banana split for your life—or do you want to settle for Satan's spinach? If you will read these pages with an open mind, there is the hope of abundant life beyond anything you've ever known. God loves you; but you must receive His love on His terms, not yours.

From Homo to Heterosexual

A true story may help here. John was twenty-two years old when I first met him in Beverly Hills, California. His father was a preacher. He came to Hollywood, running from his gay problem. He had already had some overt gay sexual experiences in college and had come to Hollywood, where he felt he would be more "accepted." John was a member of my church and was a Christian. Yes, a real Christian. A person can be a born-again child of God and still be gay. John was not a happy Christian. In fact I have yet to meet a gay person who really knows Jesus who rationalized his deviate sex life as normal. John knew he was wrong. That in itself is evidence that God's spirit in the heart of a Christian

is the spirit of truth. He will tell you the truth about God
and the gay life. John struggled with his lifestyle for two
years after I met him. We talked often about his life. He
would "go straight" for a while, then back into the gay bars
he would go, only to be grief-stricken with his guilt. He
tried to rationalize his behavior, as most gays do, but God's
love in his heart kept calling him upward to a better life.
John would not let go. Many Christian friends, girls and
guys, tried to support him in their prayers. Finally, a crisis
came. John was arrested by a plainclothesman in a hotel
men's room. He was charged with making an "approach" to
this officer. Calling me on the phone, John was a broken
man. Very ashamedly he told me he was in jail. From this
experience John agreed to call his parents and confess his
homosexuality to them. The process of healing began at this
point. John began to meet with me, with a Christian
psychiatrist (who did not rationalize and justify John's gay
life but called it what it is—sin), and with his parents, all on
a regular basis. After much prayer, repentance, and moral
support from friends in his church, John began to find deliverance. He daily prayed the only prayer a homosexual
can pray and be honest with God. John prayed for God to
give him a natural affection for women. One of John's best
friends was a pretty young actress/singer in our church. One
of the happiest days of my life was when John and his pretty
friend came to my office and announced their engagement!
That was four years ago. They now have a baby girl, and
John is the minister of music in a church. John is not gay,
but glad. Glad to be heterosexual and experiencing God's
grace. This is but one of many experiences I could share to
illustrate the power of Christ to redeem those who are lost
in the darkness of the gay world.

Witnessing to the Gay

Don't let John's experience mislead you into thinking
that it is easy to help a gay person find a restored heterosex-

ual lifestyle. It is *not* easy! In fact, it is the most difficult, heartbreaking challenge the Christian counselor will ever face. I would rather counsel the heroin addict than the gay. For every one hundred gay people you seek to help, ninety-nine will not change. The love of Jesus and the hope of heaven are not enough to persuade some to repent of this sin. It is difficult, but because Jesus cares, we must reach out to everyone who needs Him. Here then are some principles in witnessing to the gays.

THE BIBLE AND HOMOSEXUALITY

In an issue as explosive and controversial as homosexuality we must establish a point of reference. Is gay power and gay life right or wrong? If we base our answer on public opinion, there is no definite answer. Yet the Bible, *our* point of reference, is very specific on this subject. God has revealed His mind on this very clearly in His Word. His Word is timeless and His law eternal.

LEVITICUS 18:22   "You shall not lie with a male as one lies with a female; it is an abomination."

LEVITICUS 20:13   "If there is a man who lies with a male as those who lie with a woman, both of them have committed a detestable act; they shall surely be put to death."

1 CORINTHIANS 6:9, 10   "Or do you not know that the unrighteous shall not inherit the kingdom of God? Do not be deceived; neither fornicators, nor idolaters, nor adulterers, nor effeminate [by perversion], nor homosexuals . . . shall inherit the kingdom of God."

ROMANS 1:26, 27   "For this reason God gave them over to degrading passions; for their women exchanged the natural function for that which is unnatural, and in the same way also the men abandoned the natural function of the woman and burned in their desire towards one another, men with men committing indecent acts and receiving in their own persons the due penalty of their error."

What Conclusions Are Drawn From These Scriptures?

- Romans 1:26 calls lesbianism and homosexuality "unnatural." This Greek word means "against nature." It contradicts God's plan for male and female.
- Romans 1:27 calls homosexuality an indecent act, shameless before God and man. Also, it brings its own terrible penalty to the offender.
- Leviticus 18:22 calls homosexuality an abomination.
- Leviticus 20:13 says this transgression of God's law is so serious (like adultery) as to be punished by death.
- 1 Corinthians 6:9, 10 is very specific. Paul says no homosexual shall inherit the Kingdom of God. This does not mean a homosexual cannot be forgiven, but it does assert that he needs forgiveness and deliverance. God sees homosexuality as sin—the same as fornication and adultery.

Jesus and the Gays

It is beyond me how some misguided ministers seek to justify the gay life by saying Jesus was a homosexual and had twelve gay friends for disciples. We need to remember that Paul was an apostle, just as were the others, and he condemns homosexuality as does the Old Testament Scripture. We must show the homosexual that God hates this sin just as He hates all sin. He does not hate it more than any other sin, but it is an abomination in His sight. Paul went so far as to call it a "depraved mind" (Romans 1:28).

Homosexuals Are Made, Not Born

Often the gay will respond to Scripture by saying, "It's not my fault I'm this way, I didn't ask to be born gay. Why does

God condemn me? He made me this way!" My response is, someone has his facts wrong. It is not true that people are born gay. Homosexuality is not basically a genetic or hormonal imbalance. It is not a physical dysfunction caused by a number of environmental patterns. Homosexuals are made, not born, and there is no single cause. It is not my purpose here to go into all the causes, but there is a wealth of study confirming these conclusions. For further reference, see *The Problem of Homosexuality* by Charles Berg and Cliff Allen (Citadel Press, New York; 1958).

Homosexuality: Sin, Sickness, or Sensational?

If God says homosexuality is sin, then that assumes a response to temptation on man's part. Somewhere the gay individual made a few wrong turns on the road of life. He has "gone his own way," as the Bible says. Granted the gay person may have had a distorted home life which confused his mind. Granted a dominant mother and a passive father is a "setup" for a boy to become disoriented during the first few years of life. Yet, somewhere down the line, the gay *chose* to be gay. He or she gave in to Satan's enticement. At given points in time, every homosexual made choices in that direction.

The Bible says it well: The sins of the parents are passed to the third and fourth generations (Exodus 20:5). However, none of us can blame his parents for his own wrong choices. The parents are no more responsible for the homosexual's perversions than my parents are for my lust. Each man makes his own destiny by responding to God's grace or by responding to Satan's appeals.

Homosexuality is a sickness of mind, but this does not excuse it. It was a rebellion, a sin, before it became a sickness. That's why all the counseling in the world will not help the gay person until he or she sees it as a sin against God. Repentance is the first step toward restoration.

Cultural Guilt or Conscience

Gay people have often said, "We'd be all right if straight people didn't make us feel guilty. We'd be perfectly happy if you would just not push your guilt trip off on us."

What the gay is saying is that there is nothing wrong with homosexuality. Their guilt is only cultural conditioning. This is just not true! If the gay lived in a totally permissive society (as was Sodom) he would still experience real guilt for his very real sin. Can this be demonstrated?

A Disoriented Selfhood

There is general agreement among authorities that at the root of homosexuality is self-centeredness. It has been shown conclusively that the gay mind is thoroughly self-oriented. Eugene Kaplan, author of *"Homosexuality: A Search for the Ego-Ideal,"* (*Archives of General Psychiatry,* March 1967), states that the homosexual is much like the narcissist except that the homosexual is so dissatisfied with himself that he acts out his self-image with another. This is evident by the homosexual's vanity and overconcern for his appearance. The overt homosexual is so concerned with himself that he cannot sustain a love relationship. (Troy D. Perry in the *Lord Is My Shepherd and He Knows I'm Gay* repeatedly seeks to justify homosexual life on the grounds of love. He affirms that promiscuous homosexual life is wrong. A homosexual love relationship is good.) Even his "love affairs" are highly self-motivated. Because of his terrible insecurities, he covers up, pretends, and often uses people. This is not to say that all gay people fit this mold. The homosexual can also be very kind, thoughtful, and tender. Yet real guilt is there, because we cannot love others unless we have a healthy self-image. We must love ourselves before we love others. The gay person has not "found" himself. He is lost in his self-centered world. He feels the guilt that his selfishness has brought him.

DELIVERANCE FROM HOMOSEXUALITY

Having spent this much time diagnosing the patient's problem, we can now prescribe the cure. If the gay wants help, God can deliver him and give healing to heart and mind. The homosexual needs:

A Redemptive Community   The Church must show itself as redemptive toward gay people. We are neither to condemn gay life nor to condone it. We are to open our doors to sinners of every type. Gay people are no better or worse than the rest of us sinners. You and I must first show the homosexual he is welcome in the family of God. He needs Christian friends and encouragement. He can't make it without the prayer and support of a redemptive community.

A Repentant Heart   The gay must repent of his lifestyle as sin. In genuine repentance he must seek God's grace. His prayer is: "God be merciful to me a sinner, I am lost. My homosexuality is a bondage. I need healing. Father, forgive me. Give me a new heart. By your grace give me a sexuality which can honor you. I receive Jesus Christ as Lord of my life. Lord Jesus, make me to be what You want me to be."

Renunciation of Sins   It is very helpful for the homosexual to list his past homosexual sins, and by name renounce them before God. He can ask God to free him from all past fantasies and affections.

Forgiveness   A complete break with the gay crowd is mandatory. Encourage the gay person to seek forgiveness from those with whom he has been involved. He must declare his break with the gay life. This does not mean he can't love these former friends; it just means he rejects the gay lifestyle.

Competent Counsel   Here is a very difficult problem. It is not easy to find Christian counseling which is knowledgeable about this problem. However, there are psychiatrists who are Christians who can and will help the homosexual understand himself and why he is what he is.

Encouragement   Victory won't come immediately or easily. Satan will attack repeatedly. His stronghold is the mind. The gay might slip back into his sin. God still loves him; he must be encouraged to trust Jesus to fight for him and through him.

A Word of Warning

Some, not all, homosexuality is demonic. Of course all temptation is of the devil, and to a degree everyone is demon oppressed in the sense that Satan desires to oppress and harass us. However, I have counseled with a number of gay people who just could not find victory through the above-listed steps. There was an inner compulsion beyond normal temptation. It proved to be demonic and needed a different form of counseling. I know this may sound bizarre to many readers, but it is true nonetheless. To say that some homosexuals are demonized doesn't mean they are evil, wicked people. It does mean that Satan really has a death hold on the will of an individual, and that person needs divine deliverance under the leadership of a strong Christian counselor experienced in a deliverance ministry.

Come Out, Come Out, Wherever You Are

It is hoped that this chapter will be useful in witnessing to gay people and also an encouragement to the homosexual to seek the grace of God and let Jesus the Savior come into his life to transform his inner being.

RECOMMENDED SUPPLEMENTAL READING

Homosexuality: Disease or Way of Life by Edmund Bergler, M.D. (New York: The Macmillan Company, fifth printing in 1966)

16

The ABC's of Praying for the Lost

I once heard a Bible professor in one of our Christian colleges say, "It does no good to pray for lost people. God already knows who will be saved and who will not be saved. Your prayers will in no way change His plans." I disagreed with that professor then and I disagree with him now. Praying for lost people does make a difference. Not one lost person has ever been predestined to go to hell (*see* chapter 13, "What Is Predestination?") Yet how do you pray for the lost? Is it just "God, save all the lost. Amen"? Surely there is a more effective and scriptural method of interceding for a lost world.

HEAVEN IS WAITING FOR EARTH TO PRAY

We must understand that it is God's will that we pray for the lost. He is waiting on us to join Him in interceding. God chooses to act in response to the prayers of His people. While it is true that lost people are under the wrath of God, it is also true that my prayers for the lost can stay the judgment of God.

Ezekiel 22:30 tells us that God is looking for a man to "stand in the gap" that He will not have to judge the nation. God honors the ministry of intercession. Examples of such prayers are:

Abraham's prayer for Sodom (Genesis 18)
Moses' prayer for Israel (Exodus 17)
Paul's prayer for the lost (Romans 10:1)
Jesus' prayer for the lost (John 17:20)

God answers intercessory prayers. Our prayers change lives. Our prayers cause God to act in ways He ordinarily would not act. I do not understand this fact. It is a mystery, but true nonetheless.

Moses, the Intercessor—Exodus 17

This chapter contains a vivid picture of how our prayers can change the course of history. Moses and the Israelites are engaged in battle with King Amalek at Rephidim (verse 8 ff). What is Moses' battle plan? How will he and Joshua fight this very decisive battle? In verses 9–11 we read:

So Moses said to Joshua, "Choose men for us, and go out, fight against Amalek. Tomorrow I will station myself on the top of the hill with the staff of God in my hand." And Joshua did as Moses told him, and fought against Amalek; and Moses, Aaron, and Hur went up to the top of the hill. So it came about when Moses held his hand up, that Israel prevailed, and when he let his hand down, Amalek prevailed.

What a picture of the power of intercession. When Moses raises the rod of God, Joshua prevails. When Moses tires and lowers the rod, Amalek prevails. You see, the real battle wasn't being fought down in the valley with swords and spears; the real battle was being fought by Moses up on the hill! It was a spiritual battle, and Moses' intercession put God into the fight. When God is in the fight, He always makes a difference!

The Rod of God

Don't you wish you had a rod like Moses'? That rod symbolizes the power of God committed to the hand of a man. Don't you wish God would give His power to your hand the way He did to Moses? Then you could apply that power to every needy situation. Read on! You *have* a rod of God. Your rod is prayer in Jesus' name. When we pray for lost people in Jesus' name, God goes to work fighting the battle for us. I urge you to believe this truth. When we learn to pray for lost people, they will be saved; Joshua will prevail! When we don't pray, our witness is ineffective and Amalek prevails. There is a direct connection between our life as an intercessor and our life as a victorious witness.

Intercontinental Ballistic Missile

Now, what are the basic ABC's of praying for the lost? You must learn that your prayers are like intercontinental ballistic missiles. You can aim them anywhere in the world, praying for anybody, and they will always hit the target. So, where do we aim this missile of intercessory prayer? I've labeled the targets A, B, and C so you can remember them.

FIRE IN THE DIRECTION OF THE *ADVERSARY*

Our primary target, *A*, is the Adversary, Satan. Winning lost people to Christ is like freeing captives from the enemy camp. We must first defeat the enemy before we free the captives. Our primary target is not the lost sinner, but rather the power behind the sinner. Remember, Ephesians 6:12 tells us that "our struggle is not against flesh and blood, but against the rulers, against the powers, against the world forces of this darkness, against the spiritual forces of wickedness in the heavenly places." This is why we must learn to pray for lost people wisely. Satan must be defeated. He is the Adversary. He is the one who wars against us. Our prayers are powerful weapons to tear down Satanic strongholds. You must begin by understanding the sinners' lost condition.

The Condition of the Lost Sinner

The lost sinner is bound by the Adversary.   He is in spiritual chains, held captive by the devil.

- In 2 Timothy 2:25, 26 the lost person is described as in the "snare" of the devil. It is the picture of a trapped animal. The lost man is not his own man. His will is not his own. He may think he is free, but he is deceived. His sins have enslaved and trapped him.
- Matthew 12:29 and Luke 11:21, 22 describe Satan as the "strong man" who owns the unbeliever. The lost cannot be freed until first the Strong Man is defeated.

The sinner is also blinded to the gospel.   Not only is the lost man bound in his will, he is also spiritually blind to the truth of the gospel.

- Second Corinthians 4:3, 4 says, ". . . our gospel is veiled . . . to those who are perishing, in whose case the god of this world has blinded the minds of the unbelieving, that they might not see the light of the gospel of the glory of Christ . . ."

What a horrible condition to be in! Our lost friends are like we were—bound and blind. This ought to explain why the unbeliever is not interested in spiritual things. He is blinded to truth. He just can't see it. First Corinthians 2:14 tells us that spiritual things are foolishness to him.

Only Jesus and the power of the Holy Spirit can open his eyes to the truth. This is why we must not condemn lost people. They are to be prayed for, *not condemned.*

He who is lost is in need of emancipation—his will is bound. He needs revelation—his mind is darkened, blinded. It is our privilege and responsibility to help change his condition through the power of intercessory prayer. Indeed, our witness will be ineffective until the sinner's condition is changed. He will not "hear" our words or decide for our Christ until he has been delivered from Satan's control. Prayer must preclude evangelism, because of the condition of the lost. Also, you must understand:

The Conquest of the Lord Jesus Over Satan

Jesus Christ is the victor over the god of this world. Satan is a mighty foe, but he is a defeated foe. Jesus has won the victory.

This victory is twofold:

It is an absolute victory. Hebrews 2:14 declares that Jesus died on the cross in order that "through death He might render powerless him who had the power of death, that is, the devil . . . ." First John 3:8 tells us that Jesus came for the express purpose "that He might destroy the works of the devil." Christ has won an absolute victory over the Adversary. Satan is "destroyed" and "rendered powerless." He may appear fierce as a warring lion to you, but to Jesus he is just a pussycat with all his teeth pulled!

The point of these passages (*see also* Colossians 2:14, 15) is that even though the lost are in Satan's grasp, they can be freed. They need not be lost. The victory is ours. Satan is running a bluff. If only the Church would claim the victory, we would march in and claim the spoils of war. The lost can be saved, if we would but believe the victory is won!

It is an appropriated victory. There is a catch. Even though Satan has been defeated through the death and Resurrection of the Lord Jesus, the lost are still lost. They are still captives. We must appropriate their deliverance through intercessory prayer. Satan will not release them until he is commanded to do so—in the name of the conquering Christ. Our prayers appropriate the victory.

Matthew 18:18, 19 states a tremendous prayer promise from the Lord Jesus. Christ tells us we have the power to command Satan to loose our lost friends, and the devil must obey us just as he must obey Christ:

> Truly I say to you, whatever you shall bind on earth shall have been bound in heaven; and whatever you loose on earth shall have been loosed in heaven.

> Again I say to you, that if two of you agree on earth about anything that they may ask, it shall be done for them by My Father who is in heaven.

What does this passage promise? It says anything that has *already* been bound in heaven (note that the verb is perfect, passive) we can bind here on earth through prayer in Jesus' name. Now, what does that mean? Has Satan been bound in heaven? Yes, he has! Hebrews 1:13 says Jesus has His foot on Satan's head! That is a picture of total victory. Therefore, you can bind him on earth. You can command Satan to stop his attack on your lost friend. Each prayer you pray can be a liberating force in your friend's life. You can "loose" your lost friend from Satan's binding and blinding. His will can be freed, his mind enlightened to the gospel through your prayers; he or she can make a response to Christ. What a weapon is intercessory prayer! It is a tragedy that prayer is so seldom used and so few believers know how to use it against the enemy.

So here is the A of praying for lost people. When you pray for the lost, you must first deal with the devil, just as Jesus did. You must rebuke Satan *first*. In praying for the lost, you must rebuke Satan, commanding him to release the captive. You keep on rebuking, day after day, until that person is saved.

Learn to claim the work of Calvary in the lost one's life. As you rebuke the Adversary, remember that you have every right to demand that he release your lost friend. Jesus has purchased this redemption for all men. His blood has paid the ransom to deliver the lost. The lost are no longer Satan's property, they are Christ's. So, pray in authority, pray in faith, assaulting the Gates of Hell, demanding that Satan release the property that belongs to Jesus. Sign your command "in Jesus' name." Satan must honor that IOU. Believe it. Claim it. Pray it!

PRAY IN THE DIRECTION OF THE *BELIEVERS*

Now we come to *B* of the ABC's of praying for the lost. When we have dealt with the devil, we are to ask God to send a witness to our friend. Each day, we pray asking the Father to send believers as a testimony to our friend. This Jesus commanded us to do in Matthew 9:38.

We are praying for God to send a prepared saint to a prepared sinner. This is the way God does things. This is His pattern for evangelism. In Acts 8 there is a good example of this truth. The African eunuch is searching the Scriptures. He is reading Isaiah 53. He cannot understand it. He is ready to be saved. He is willing. Then God sends Phillip to him with the message of Christ. Acts 10 also illustrates this truth. Cornelius, a Roman, is ready to hear the gospel. God sends Peter to him that he might be saved.

Therefore, as I pray for the lost, I first rebuke the devil for this day in the life of the person I am interceding for. Then, I ask the Father to send a witness to him when he is ready. It may be a radio preacher as he drives to work, a Gideon Bible in a motel room, a Christian at the office; I don't know how God will do it, but He will send a witness to my friend—somehow. Count on it. Believe it.

PRAY IN THE DIRECTION OF *CHRIST*

I hope you can see that praying for the lost is not a matter of begging a reluctant God to please spare lost people. He is willing and able. Often He is just waiting for us to ask. It is now time for us to claim Christ's promise in John 14:14. He promised that "if you ask Me anything in My name, I will do it." The phrase in this verse that excites me is "*I will do it.*" Jesus Himself will do it. When you pray, ask Jesus Himself, through His Holy Spirit, to go to your lost friend. Jesus can knock on the door of the heart and confront the sinner.

My Prayers Put Jesus to Work

This is an amazing truth. Your prayers put Jesus Christ to work in the life of the lost people. He is the Lord of the harvest (Matthew 9:38). His Spirit can convince the lost of the need to be saved. This thrills my heart. I can pray for a lost person halfway around the world, and Jesus will go to that person immediately in answer to my prayer. That ought to encourage us to pray more!

A PRACTICAL GUIDE TO INTERCESSORY PRAYER FOR THE LOST

Let me suggest that as you regularly pray for certain people, you follow these simple ABC's of prayer.

Rebuke the Adversary

Pray: "Satan, I come against you in behalf of my friend _____. In the name of Jesus the Christ, I command you to loose him today. You have no right to him. He belongs to the Lord Jesus, and I am claiming his salvation in Jesus' name."

You must do battle day after day until salvation comes. Take heart; when Satan realizes you mean business, he will back off. However, he will not obey if your faith is weak and your intercessions are not continuous.

Request God to Send Believers

Pray: "Father send a witness today to my friend. Surround him with Your love. Bring some human influence into his life that will bring him closer to You."

Request the Holy Spirit to Convict

Now ask Jesus to come to him this day. Pray:

"Lord Jesus, I ask You to knock on his heart. Show him Your love; open his eyes to the truth. Speak to him today."

Thank God for His Salvation

Claim 1 John 5:14. Believe your friend *is being saved.* Thank the Father in advance for saving your friend. Leave the *when* and *how* up to God. Let God do it His way and in His own time—but ask and keep on asking, knock and keep on knocking, and the lost will be saved.

17

What Is Happiness?

Happiness Is Different Things to Different People:

> to a college student it may be . . .
> a game played and won
> or a song well sung
>
> or it may be
> graduation in spring
> or a girl with a ring
>
> or to some happiness is
> a night of sin
> and thrills to the end.

Yes, happiness means different things to different people—*but what if there is more to happiness than things, events, or human relationships?* What if these things are not really happiness at all?

There are so many people today who are unhappy. The Bible gives us a clue. God's Word says you were created for a specific purpose. Because there is only one basic purpose for human life, there is only one road to happiness!

What is the basic purpose God has for your life?

> Thou art worthy, O Lord, to receive glory and honour
> and power: for thou hast created all things, and for
> thy pleasure they are and were created.
>
> Revelation 4:11 KJV

Here is the key to meaningful living. Happiness comes from pleasing God with your life. All things were created to glorify the Creator. This verse tells us four things about why we exist:

- God is the Creator of all things—including you!
- God, because of who He is, is worthy to receive glory, honor, and authority.
- God created all things for the express purpose of giving Him glory, honor, and power.
- You were created to bring glory to God; this is God's will for every created thing.

WHAT DOES GOD SAY HAPPINESS IS?

Happiness is the result of being what you were created to be and doing what you were created to do.

The world of nature illustrates this truth in that all of nature glorifies Creator-God.

We often speak of "Mother Nature," because nature demands a first cause to account for its existence.

There is one created being that does not glorify God: man! Mankind lives for self-glory and self-pleasure.

How can I please God and as a result live a full and meaningful life?

> They said therefore to Him, "What shall we do, that we may work the works of God?"
>
> John 6:28

These men were asking the great religious question: What must I do to please God? What must I do to glorify God and therefore live a purposeful, happy life?

Jesus gave an astonishing answer:

> This is the work of God, that you believe in Him whom He has sent.
>
> John 6:29

Note Jesus said if you want to please God and be happy, there aren't many things you must do—only one thing: *Believe in Me!*

Now that's amazing. Simply believe in Jesus Christ and you'll glorify God and live life with a capital *L*!

Why must you believe in Jesus Christ to live an abundant life?

> . . . I do nothing on My own initiative, but I speak these things as the Father taught Me . . . . for I always do the things that are pleasing to Him.
>
> John 8:28, 29

Jesus Christ is the only man who has always pleased God! He is the sinless, only begotten Son of God. He has pleased God for us. He is our substitute. He came to live for us, and to die for us!

> The wages of sin is death, but the free gift of God is eternal life in Christ Jesus our Lord.
>
> Romans 6:23

His death and Resurrection are God's offer of a second chance for you. Jesus Christ, through the Holy Spirit, wants to live His perfect life in and through you to the glory of God. *Believing is receiving. The Christ-controlled life is the happy life. Will you let Jesus make you happy?*

> But as many as received him, to them gave he power to become the sons of God, even to them that believe on his name.
>
> John 1:12 KJV

When you receive the Holy Spirit, Jesus comes into you to live your life for you. He will glorify the Father through you.

- You were created to live for God's glory.
- You have lived for self and self-glory (the basis of all sin).
- Jesus Christ is God's offer of forgiveness and abundant life.
- You must personally receive God's offer by inviting Jesus Christ into your life.

WHAT MUST I DO TO BE SAVED?

- Admit your need of Him.
- Be willing to turn from your sin and self. (Christ will help you once you turn to Him.)
- Believe Jesus died for you.
- Invite Him into your life.

For whosoever shall call upon the name of the Lord shall be saved.

Romans 10:13 KJV

HOW DO I PRAY TO BE SAVED?

Remember that becoming a real Christian is not just saying words but receiving a person—the Lord Jesus. Pray this prayer:

Dear Lord, I know I have done wrong. I am willing to turn from my sins. I believe Jesus Christ died for me. Please come into my life and forgive me of my sins. I receive You into my life as my Lord and Savior, as best I know how right now. Amen.

Did you ask Christ to forgive you of your sins and come into your life? Did you mean it? What happened?

And this is the record, that God hath given to us eternal life, and this life is in his Son. He that hath the Son hath life; and he that hath not the Son of God hath not life. These things have I written unto you that believe on the name of the Son of God; that ye may know that ye have eternal life . . . .

1 John 5:11–13 KJV

Jesus said:

. . . and him that cometh to me I will in no wise cast out.

John 6:37 KJV

Believe God and His Word, not your feelings.

WELCOME TO GOD'S FAMILY

Now that you have been spiritually born, you need spiritual food for growth in the Christian life. To assure growth you should:

- Fellowship with the Father by reading His Word (the Bible) every day (1 Peter 2:2).
- Meet Him in prayer every day (Matthew 7:7, 8).
- Fellowship, worship, and serve the Father with other Christians in a church where Christ is preached (Hebrews 10:25).
- Tell others about Christ (1 John 1:3).
- Perform a ministry in the world by loving others in Christ's name (Mark 9:41).

Index